The Whole Child

A Caregiver's Guide
To The First Five Years

Student Guide
for the Seventh Edition

By Patricia Weissman, Ed.D., Judith Allen Kaminsky and Joanne Hendrick, Ph.D.
Revised by Joanne Hendrick, Ph.D.

The Whole Child: A Caregiver's Guide to the First Five Years
is produced by
Detroit Public Television (WTVS) in association with the
Merrill-Palmer Institute of Wayne State University.

This *Student Guide* for *The Whole Child: A Caregiver's Guide to the First Five Years* has been updated to correspond to *The Whole Child: Developmental Education for the Early Years*, Seventh Edition, by Joanne Hendrick, Ph.D., of the University of Oklahoma, published by Merrill/Prentice Hall.

Funding for
The Whole Child: A Caregiver's Guide to the First Five Years
is provided by Annenberg/CPB.

Annenberg/CPB, a partnership between the Annenberg Foundation and the Corporation for Public Broadcasting, uses media and telecommunications to advance excellent teaching in American schools. Annenberg/CPB funds educational series and teacher professional development workshops for the Annenberg/CPB Channel. The Channel is distributed free by satellite to schools and to other educational and community organizations nationwide.

To purchase copies of Annenberg/CPB videos and guides, or to learn more about other professional development materials and the Annenberg/CPB Channel, contact Annenberg/CPB by phone, by mail, or on the Web.

▲ Annenberg/CPB

P. O. Box 2345
S. Burlington, Vermont 05407-2345

1-800-LEARNER

info@learner.org
www.learner.org

Additional funding for *The Whole Child: A Caregiver's Guide to the First Five Years* was provided by the Charles Stewart Mott Foundation of Flint, Michigan.

Cover image created by Grace and Wild Digital Studios, Farmington Hills, Michigan.

ISBN: 0-13-095078-5   4 5   05 04

The Merrill-Palmer Institute

Wayne State University

2 the whole child student guide

welcome

This *Student Guide* is designed to make the most of a terrific textbook, and a remarkable series of television programs which were shot in a dozen working child care centers and family care homes and illustrate the important lessons of the text.

Read the following **introduction** to find out all the features of this *Guide,* and how to make the most of the course.

If you have questions about the Spanish-language materials, videocassettes, the *Parent Guide* for this series, the project Web site or other courses from the Annenberg/CPB Multimedia Collection, contact:

THE WHOLE CHILD
The Annenberg/CPB Multimedia Collection
P.O. Box 2345
South Burlington, VT 05407-2345
1-800-LEARNER
www.learner.org

If you have questions about the textbook or English-language Student Guide, please contact:

Merrill Education/Prentice Hall
445 Hutchinson Ave.
Columbus, OH 43235
1-800-228-7854
www.merrilleducation.com

[CC] This series is closed-captioned in English for the hearing-impaired.

thank yous

We owe a lot to the parents and children who allowed us to videotape them through all the normal ups and downs of many days. We are especially grateful for the staff members at these centers who put their child care practice under the unblinking scrutiny of the television lens so others could learn from what they do.

The Bussey Center
Southfield, MI

The Child Development Center
The University of Michigan-Dearborn
Dearborn, MI

Compuware Child Development Center
Farmington Hills, MI

Epoch Child Care Center, Inc.
Detroit, MI

Gwen Wright's Nurture Place Daycare
Detroit, MI

Human Services Department
Detroit Head Start Program

Kresge Early Childhood Development Program
Southfield, MI

Lil' Tykes Learning Center
Livonia, MI

Poe School
Detroit, MI

Rena's Childcare
D.B.A. Happy Days Nursery
West Bloomfield, MI

Vistas Nuevas
St. Gabriel Head Start
Detroit, MI

Wayne State University
College of Education
Early Childhood Center
Detroit, MI

A special thanks to the person who pulled us all together in the first place, and gave us the charge to create something truly excellent:

Eli Saltz, Ph.D.
Director
Merrill-Palmer Institute
Wayne State University

Our outstanding advisory council gave us invaluable advice and encouragement throughout the development of the television series and all the related material. They are a terrific group of teachers who guided us through our own "emergent" curriculum.

Ruby Burgess, Ph.D.
Chair, Department of Education
Winston-Salem State University

Kathleen Alison Clarke-Stewart, Ph.D.
Professor of Psychology and Social Behavior
School of Social Ecology
University of California, Irvine

Joan Costley
Senior Fellow
The Center for Career Development in
Early Care and Education
Wheelock College
Boston, MA

Adrienne Garcia, Ph.D.
Executive Director
H. Lee Moffitt Cancer Center and Research
Institute Foundation, Inc.
Tampa, FL

Frederick L. Goodman, Ph.D.
Professor of Education
The University of Michigan

Barbara Ferguson Kamara, M.S.
Executive Director
Office of Early Childhood Development
Washington, DC

Lilian Katz, Ph.D.
Professor
College of Education
University of Illinois, Urbana-Champaign

Michael D. Lougee, Ph.D.
Senior Research Associate
Schools of Education and Medicine
The University of Michigan

Carol B. Phillips, Ph.D.
Executive Director
Council for Early Childhood
Professional Recognition
Washington, DC

Rosalyn Saltz, Ph.D.
Professor of Education, Emerita
University of Michigan-Dearborn

Irving Sigel, Ph.D.
Distinguished Research
Psychologist, Emeritus
Educational Testing Service
Princeton, NJ

Jane Squires, Ph.D.
Professor
Center on Human Development
College of Education
University of Oregon

Dora Pulido Tobiassen
Project Associate
California Tomorrow
San Francisco, CA

Our evaluation team gave us great feedback
from teachers, students and parents who will
be using our course:

Rita Richey, Ph.D.
School of Education
Wayne State University

Alvin L. Edelson, Ph.D.
School of Education
Wayne State University

Our production team was led by:

Harvey Ovshinsky
Executive Producer
HKO Media, Inc., Grosse Pointe, MI

Joanne Hendrick, Ph.D.
Author of *The Whole Child*
Series Host and Content Consultant
Professor of Early Childhood Education,
    Emerita
University of Oklahoma

Patricia Weissman, Ed.D.
Early Childhood Content
Coordinator/Research Associate
Merrill-Palmer Institute
Wayne State University

Judith Allen Kaminsky
Instructional Designer
Merrill-Palmer Institute
Wayne State University

Darryl Wood
Series Senior Producer
Detroit Public Television

James Woods
Series Director
Detroit Public Television

Tracey Talkington
Associate Producer
Detroit Public Television

Thank you all.

Bob Rossbach
Executive in Charge of Production
Project Director
Detroit Public Television

table of contents and course outline

social development

fostering emergent curriculum and cognitive development

introduction to the *student guide*

"getting started"

THE WHOLE CHILD: THE CAREGIVER'S GUIDE TO THE FIRST FIVE YEARS is an innovative curriculum that provides an ideal learning environment for the self-motivated student: the structure and content of a university course; the visual, practical experience of viewing real situations in different types of child care centers with all kinds of children; and the independence to complete the course in the student's own time at home. Because telecourse use is new to many students, this section addresses ways you can learn from the video programs and integrate their use with that of the text and *Student Guide*.

The video programs in each unit of **THE WHOLE CHILD** curriculum are designed to "bring the text to life." In them, Dr. Joanne Hendrick, author of *The Whole Child*, outlines the most important principles covered in the relevant chapters. Through discussion and the use of bullet points, Dr. Hendrick emphasizes the theories and philosophies behind her positive approach to foster the development of the five selves of the whole child: physical, emotional, social, creative and cognitive. Practical ways to implement this approach are outlined by Dr. Hendrick and then illustrated though real situations in scenes videotaped at a number of different child care centers. These are real scenes from a diverse group of infant centers and preschools. The video programs show positive environments, teaching approaches and activities as well as examples of interactions that teachers would handle differently the next time. Discussions among teachers and caregivers about their experiences as well as parent-teacher interaction are included and teachers are shown learning about children through observation and active listening.

interacting with the video program

Of primary importance is the opportunity for reflection provided by **THE WHOLE CHILD** curriculum. These video programs have been designed to stimulate thought among students who are likely to experience similar real-life situations. Try to brainstorm answers to questions asked in the video program or solutions to problems presented. When examples of desirable and less successful approaches are shown, think of similar situations from your practical experiences. Try to think of multiple solutions to the predicaments encountered by teachers and caregivers in the video program. These situational experiences will also challenge you to think about what your own responses would be. As a result, you may be able to think of ways to improve the environment at the center where you are currently working or observing. The video programs also give you the opportunity to re-evaluate an activity, approach or interaction from your experience. Take time for personal reflections regarding your own philosophy and possible concerns about being a teacher and caregiver. Reflection can be used as a self-referencing tool, a process of relating the information presented in this course to your own experiences.

Through participation and generating your own ideas, you will be able to fully understand important educational principles and integrate them into your own unique teaching style. Use this interactive potential in any way that is possible. Discussion and role playing with friends, family members, a student study partner or study group will contribute to a more thorough understanding of the principles and approaches presented in this course. Try to role play ways to handle the difficult situations presented in the video programs. When the video programs present questions or dilemmas and another person is not available for discussion and role play, answer aloud to yourself or in written form.

distance learners

The *Student Guide* is designed as a workbook with particular attention to the distance learner who is taking this course at home. Each unit of the *Student Guide* also includes a **Unit Overview**, list of **Unit Objectives, Focus for Learning,** set of **Video-Related Questions for Reflection and Role Playing** and several **Predicaments for Your Consideration. Assignments for Students Working or Volunteering with Children** are included as well as **Observational Assignments** for those who have little experience with children. It will be very beneficial for you to become involved in interacting with children before beginning this course. If not currently working in a child care center, try to volunteer or at least observe in some setting with preschool children. Even a regular baby-sitting job would give you opportunities to observe children and practice the approaches presented in the text and video programs.

Taking a telecourse on your own has many advantages. You can work at your own pace and at times convenient for you and your family. However, it is important for you to be exceptionally well-organized and self-disciplined because successful completion requires that you use all components of the telecourse as stipulated by the instructor and *Student Guide.* Keep up with the course on a weekly basis by reading text assignments and viewing video programs on a regular schedule. Video programs may be broadcast on one or more local public TV stations, on cable and/or on a closed circuit network run by the college or university. Video programs may also be available on video cassette at the college library, either for viewing there or borrowing. Your telecourse instructor will advise you about which options exist. Set a schedule for viewing and stick to it. Try to complete all assignments and examinations according to the guidelines given by your instructor.

Keep in close contact with your instructor in person during office hours, by phone, e-mail or regular mail. Your instructor can assist students having difficulty understanding the course material and with questions about the principles or approaches presented. Your instructor is also an important source of interaction when you need to clarify or discuss course content.

It is important for you to attend the orientation session and any additional discussion or review sessions offered by your instructor. These opportunities for interaction contribute greatly to your understanding of the course material. These sessions also enable you to meet other students taking the course in order to find study partners or form study groups. Although it is possible to do all the distance learning on your own, it is a lot more satisfying to view the video programs and share your ideas about them together whenever you can arrange to do this.

steps for each lesson

The *Student Guide* is designed to help you evaluate and develop what you view and read by reinforcing key concepts and themes. The Student Guide is meant to be a tutor in book form, a means of organizing disparate information into a coherent learning experience. If you follow these steps, you should find that you thoroughly understand the principles and approaches presented in **THE WHOLE CHILD** curriculum.

1. First read the **Unit Overview** and **Unit Objectives** in the appropriate unit of the *Student Guide*. Reading through the overview and objectives will give you a sense of the scope of the material in the text chapter(s) and video program.

2. Next read the **Text Assignment** chapter(s). Make pencil markings beside the paragraphs or sentences that you feel are most important. Pencil markings allow you to change your emphasis as needed. Then reread the passages you have marked. Answer the **Self-Check Questions For Review** that are listed for each chapter.

3. Read the **Focus for Learning** sectionand the **Video-Related Questions for Reflection and Role Play** before you watch each unit's video program. This will give you an idea of what you can expect to see emphasized by Dr. Hendrick and illustrated in the various child care centers.

4. Then watch **THE WHOLE CHILD** video program for that unit. View these programs actively. Take notes in your journal on the key points. After viewing the video program, respond to each of the **Video-Related Questions for Reflection and Role Play** by interacting with another person, aloud to yourself or in your journal. Try to find opportunities to role play various approaches in different types of situations with a friend, family member or student study partner. If working or volunteering in any setting with children, practice what you have learned and experienced from the text and video program. Active involvement and participation will enhance your

learning substantially and increase your comfort level as you develop your own style of interacting with children.

5. Read the **Predicaments for Your Consideration**. Answer each of these aloud to yourself or in writing. This exercise is very valuable because it provides you with realistic situations that are commonly encountered in child care centers. Be sure your answers are complete and would help to resolve the predicament, based on all that you have learned in the text and video program. Where possible, stretch your thinking by proposing more than one way to solve the predicament. Instructors may require use of a journal in responding to these predicaments.

6. If you are currently working or volunteering in a child care setting, complete the **Assignments for Students Working or Volunteering With Children** that your instructor has chosen. Make sure that your written responses to these assignments are thorough. Submit these to your instructor.

7. Complete the **Observational Assignments** that your instructor has chosen. These assignments are meant to provide you with an opportunity to observe children in order to contribute to your understanding of the course content. The written response to these assignments should be submitted to your instructor.

8. If you would like to test yourself to see how you're doing, take a minute to check out *The Whole Child* Web site. It offers self-test questions for each chapter of the book. You can find it at www.prenhall.com/hendrick. Or, if you prefer, check out the TV series Web site at www.pbs.org/wholechild.

notes

unit 1
handling daily routines

video program: *it's the little things*

handling daily routines

unit overview

Read this section before reading the text assignr.:ent.

Children thrive in a well-ordered and predictable environment, where such things as arrivals and departures, mealtimes, nap times and toileting are dealt with consistently by all caregivers, both parents and professionals. In this unit, you will study the importance of plans and schedules, as well as what to expect at certain stages of a child's development. The intent of this unit is to equip you with techniques for helping children move easily and comfortably through the routines of the center day and also acquaint you with the educational purposes and goals that underlie current practice. Beneficial ways of carrying out routines so they foster emotional health and stability in the children are emphasized.

unit objectives

Read these objectives before reading the text assignment.

THIS UNIT:

1. Helps you understand the general principles related to handling routines in a healthy way.

2. Acquaints you with the elements of a good, full-day schedule.

3. Provides strategies for carrying through smooth transitions.

4. Sensitizes you to the need for handling parent-child separations gently.

5. Informs you about sound nutritional planning that incorporates multicultural values and makes mealtime a pleasure for everyone.

6. Informs you about what constitutes wholesome attitudes toward toileting and nap time.

text assignment

Read this assignment.

Chapter 4, "Handling Daily Routines," *The Whole Child*, Seventh Edition, Joanne Hendrick.

*Refer to **Self-Check Questions for Review**.*

Chapter 4, p. 102.

focus for learning

Read this section before viewing the video program.

Emphasize the importance of maintaining a reasonable balance between conformity to group procedures and adjustment to individual needs of children. It is also helpful to spend considerable time on what-to-do-when situations as well as using reflection to consider deeply embedded convictions of what you may feel to be the "right" way or the "wrong" way to handle toileting, eating and so forth.

The video program, *It's the Little Things,* can be a valuable tool in promoting thought and stimulating ideas for role playing and practical experience. Use the following section of **Video-Related Questions** to help you begin to think about some of the important issues that the video program will address. That way, when similar questions are posed in the video program, you can begin to think about what your responses might be. Being an active viewer of the video program will help you to respond to the following **Video-Related Questions for Reflection and Role Play** in a more thoughtful way.

video-related questions for reflection and role play

Read these questions before viewing the video program. After viewing the program, respond to the questions assigned by your instructor by interacting with another person, aloud to yourself or in your journal. Try to find opportunities to role play or practice the approaches illustrated.

1. What experiences have you had with separation anxiety among infants, toddlers or preschool children? What approaches worked the best to help the child and the parents with this adjustment? Try to brainstorm ways to reduce the uncertainty the child feels in this situation. Find opportunities to role play interacting with children and parents. You can draw on experience you may have had baby-sitting small children. What special challenges are presented when children speak other languages in a situation like this? How can teachers help these children to feel comfortable in a new classroom?

2. Reflect on and find opportunities to discuss with another student how children's center schedules can be evaluated to insure a balance between conformity to group procedures and individual needs. How would you determine if a schedule is providing enough time for children to become deeply involved in their play?

3. What experiences have you had with infant caregiving? How do you feel about talking to infants about what is happening and going to happen next? What do you feel is the value of responding to the sounds that infants make? How realistic do you feel it is to feed infants on demand in an infant center setting? Is there any reason to be concerned about using food as a pacifier for infants?

4. Find opportunities to practice facilitating smooth transitions in a preschool classroom. You may be able to get inspiration and ideas from your own experiences or from the video program. Learn to warn once in advance and make a positive comment about the next activity. You may find that you have to allow the "child" to finish what she is doing or talk about a later time when the "child" can finish her work.

5. What do you feel is the best way to determine the eating preferences and habits of the children who may be in a class you are teaching. These preferences and habits may be tied to culture, religion, allergies, family lifestyle and/or the child's own taste. Try to reflect on or discuss the challenge of feeding a group of children who may have different eating restrictions or preferences.

6. Find role playing opportunities that encourage dialogue among the children at the lunch table. Try to think of interesting, substantive subjects which will foster conversation *among the children*.

7. Reflect on or discuss any discomfort or reluctance you might feel about dealing with toileting and young children. How do you feel about allowing

children of different genders to toilet together? How do you feel about discussing gender differences with young children? Do you feel that family and cultural differences would be a factor in toileting in general and allowing children of different genders to toilet together?

8. Reflect on or discuss reasons why children may have difficulty settling down at nap time. Brainstorm ways that you could help children relax and rest for a period of time. Have you had any opportunities to develop your own "bag of tricks" through baby-sitting or work in a child care center?

9. Think about different types of disabilities that preschool children may have. Then reflect on or discuss special considerations that you would need to make, as a teacher, when approaching different routines such as separation, transitions, mealtime, nap time and toileting. Special considerations might include: teaching of skills, timing, room arrangement, consultation with parents of a child with disability and discussion with other children and their parents.

predicaments for your consideration

Respond to the predicaments assigned by your instructor with another person, aloud to yourself or in your journal.

1. You are the staff teacher who greets children at the door every morning and there is one little boy, fairly new to the school, who always begins to whimper as he arrives. The boy's father usually tries to ignore him and makes light of the situation. Today, the father gets upset and gives the child a smack on the bottom, telling him firmly, "This has gone on long enough! It's time to be tough! Anyway, little boys don't cry!" You have learned in your student teaching days that it is important for children to express their feelings. How would you handle this situation? How could you let the father know that his son's reaction to separation and a new school is very healthy? How can you help the child to feel more comfortable and secure in this new setting?

2. Although you never meant to have things arrive at such an impasse, you have inadvertently made such an issue of a child's going to the toilet that she will not use the toilet anymore and wets her pants instead. At this point, what approach would you try next to solve this difficulty? How can you work with the child's family in a situation like this?

assignments for students working or volunteering with children

Complete this assignment and submit the written response to your instructor.

Plan a lunch menu for the center where you are working that includes one dish from an ethnic group represented by the children in your classroom. Make sure your menu meets the School Lunch Requirements of the U.S. Department of Agriculture. Ask the children and parents for help in choosing the dish and recipe. Ethnic cookbooks may also be useful.

Plan a day for this lunch to be served. Ask children and parents to help in preparing this special dish. Children can tell the others the name of their dish and describe the ingredients.

WRITTEN ASSIGNMENT

Describe the cultural origins of the dish and how nutritional requirements were met with your menu. Describe how you chose the dish, where you got the recipe and how children and parents contributed in preparing the meal. Then describe the reactions of the children to the unfamiliar food and your overall impressions of the experience. How did the families respond to this activity?

observational assignment

Complete this assignment and submit the written response to your instructor.

Try to observe in a preschool classroom for a whole morning or afternoon. Evaluate how realistic the schedule is for the children in the class. Consider the following questions: Are activity times long enough to allow children to involve themselves deeply in their play? Did you observe any instances when the schedule was altered in response to the interests or activities of the children? Is enough time allotted for transitions? How smoothly do children change from one activity to another? How do teachers handle any children who are resistant to changing their activity? How do teachers handle clean-up?

Take notes on these questions and any other observations you made on the subject of center schedules and transitions while in the classroom. Then write up your observations and suggest ways that the schedule, transitions and clean-up could be improved.

references for further reading

Berman, C., & Fromer, J. (1991). *Meals Without Squeals*. Palo Alto, CA: Bull.

Cox, B., & Jacobs, M. (1991). *Spirit of the Harvest: North American Indian Cooking*. New York: Stewart, Tabori, & Chang.

Crocker, B. (1993). *Betty Crocker's Mexican Made Easy*. Upper Saddle River, NJ: Prentice Hall.

Cryer, D., Ray, A.R., & Harms, T. (1996). *Nutrition Activities for Preschoolers*. Menlo Park, CA: Addison-Wesley.

Katzen, M., & Henderson, A. (1994). *Pretend Soup and Other Real Recipes: A Cookbook for Preschoolers and Up*. Berkley, CA: Tricycle Press.

Larson, N., Henthorne, M., & Plum, B. (1994). *Transition Magician: Strategies for Guiding Young Children in Early Childhood Programs*. St. Paul, MN: Redleaf.

Parham, V.R. (1993). *The African American Child's Heritage Cookbook*. South Pasadena, CA: Sandcastle.

Wilson, M. (1989). *The Good-for-Your-Health All-Asian Cookbook*. Washington, DC: Center for Science in the Public Interest.

notes

unit 2
development of the
physical self

video program: *by leaps and bounds*

development of the physical self

unit overview

Read this section before reading the text assignment.

This unit offers an overview of typical physical development in early childhood, including the development of children's large muscle, fine muscle and perceptual-motor skills. This unit also provides a framework for planning a comprehensive range of activities that fosters the full physical development of each child. You will learn how to follow good health practices, and how to provide a secure environment and safe activities that will help bring the children's physical development to its fullest potential.

unit objectives

Read these objectives before reading the text assignment.

THIS UNIT:

1. Emphasizes the value of good physical health and the importance of the teacher's role in monitoring that state in the children.
2. Builds an appreciation of the value of physical activities for young children.
3. Provides an outline for planning developmentally appropriate activities that provide comprehensive coverage for physical development.
4. Builds an appreciation of the value of sensory experience in the life of the child.

text assignment

Read this assignment.

Chapter 5, "Development of the Physical Self," *The Whole Child*, Seventh Edition, Joanne Hendrick.

Refer to Self-Check Questions for Review.

Chapter 5, p. 129.

focus for learning

One interesting question to explore is the value of structured versus nonstructured physical activities and how children might benefit from both possibilities. Try to reflect on what constitutes a reasonable balance between concern for potentially dangerous situations and overprotection or overrestriction of children's creative activities. Find opportunities to discuss the importance of physically expressing affection to children through hugging and touching as well as any reluctance that you or fellow students may have because of the fear of sexual abuse accusations.

The video program, *By Leaps and Bounds*, can be a valuable tool in promoting thought and stimulating ideas for role playing and practical experience. Use the following section of **Video-Related Questions** to help you begin to think about some of the important issues that the video program will address. That way, when similar questions are posed in the video program, you can begin to think about what your responses might be. Being an active viewer of the video program will help you to respond to the following **Video-Related Questions for Reflection and Role Play** in a more thoughtful way.

video-related questions for reflection and role play

Read these questions before viewing the video program. After viewing the program, respond to the questions assigned by your instructor by interacting with another person, aloud to yourself or in your journal. Try to find opportunities to role play or practice the approaches illustrated.

1. What activities would allow infants to practice physical skills they already have and challenge them to develop new skills? Brainstorm activities other than those shown in the video program.

2. Think of examples from your practical experience when a decision had to be made whether a child's activity was dangerous or not. Did the adult stop the activity or did she determine that the child was able to try out something new and experiment with a piece of equipment or other activity?

3. What creative outside activities can you offer children to challenge and enhance their creative abilities? Brainstorm ideas other than those shown in the video program or described in the teacher testimonials. Ideas can center around equipment that allows children to test their strength and make discoveries about the physical properties the equipment possesses.

4. Think of different types of materials that would offer children two levels of difficulty in the development of their fine muscle skills, i.e., large and small wooden beads, two puzzles with the same picture but different number of pieces. This offers children the opportunity to move on to a more challenging activity after they have mastered a simpler one.

5. What ideas do you have for sensory activities that compare substances according to the way they smell and feel? What interesting substances can be used and how would you present this activity? How would you present an activity that helps children develop their ability to tell sounds apart? What materials could be used for this activity?

6. Brainstorm ways to teach children to relax through new and interesting activities. How do you relax and can this knowledge help you to develop relaxation activities for children?

7. Think about how you would react to a family who feels that physical expression of affection (hugging, touching) is harmful to their 4 year-old son's healthy development and is contrary to the beliefs of their cultural heritage. How would you explain the value of physical affection for young children without offending this family?

8. Think of two large muscle activities that can be offered to a child with a physical disability who is confined to a wheelchair. What are two large muscle activities that can be offered to a child with Down Syndrome who is very active yet may need extra guidance to participate in the activity?

9. Do you thoroughly understand what it means to follow "universal precautions"? What exactly are these procedures and why are they important? What kinds of health precautions would you recommend for the situations in this video, i.e., science experiment, infants mouthing toys, handling of food?

predicaments for your consideration

Respond to the predicaments assigned by your instructor with another person, aloud to yourself or in your journal.

1. You are the director of a children's center and you have just admitted Jason, who uses a wheelchair, to the 3 year-old class. In order to include him in all the activities, you know some physical changes will have to be made in the school. To your delight, the child's father is good at building things and has said he would be happy to help any way he can. You have called a conference with Jason's parents and teachers to talk over what adjustments should be made. In order to get things started, you have thought of several possibilities yourself. Suggest what these possibilities might include.

2. A little girl has just fallen out of the swing and is brought into the office bleeding heavily from the mouth. Examination reveals that her front tooth is still whole but has cut entirely through her lower lip. As the teacher in charge, how would you handle this emergency? Remember to think about both short- and long-terms aspects of the situation.

3. You are now the director of a child care center, and the annual visit by the licensing agency is due very soon. When you check the immunization records of the children in preparation for that visit, to your surprise you find that about a third of the children's immunizations are not up-to-date. You send out a notice requesting parents to take the children to the doctor to have the necessary shots. Three weeks later, only two parents have turned in updated reports. What steps would you take next to ensure compliance with the regulations?

assignment for students working or volunteering with children

Complete this assignment and submit the written response to your instructor.

Plan the physical development activities for the outdoor play area for an entire week at the center where you are working. Be sure to include all eight categories of physical activities: locomotion, balance (static and dynamic), body and space perception, rhythm and temporal awareness, rebound and airborne activities, projectile management, fine muscle activities and relaxation activities. Plan an activity from each category at least twice during the week. Be sure to include opportunities for the children to practice relaxation activities. Work with the teachers at your center and try to make your plan a part of the center curriculum for a particular week.

If your plan was used at the center, evaluate the results when the week was over.

1. Were all the categories covered with appropriate activities at least twice during the week?

2. Were all the activities safe?

3. Did they provide enough range of difficulty so that more and less skilled children were attracted to them and could participate?

4. What activities were changed as a result of the children's ideas and suggestions?

5. What were the particular strong points of the activities you selected?

6. What will you change the next time you are in charge of planning this area?

observational assignment

Complete this assignment and submit your written response to your instructor.

Make arrangements to observe in a preschool classroom for a whole morning, afternoon or even a full day, if possible. See how many examples of perceptual-motor activities (locomotion, balance, body and space perception, rhythm and temporal awareness, rebound and airborne activities, projectile management, daily motor activities including fine muscle tasks, relaxation activities) you can observe and make note of during your visit. Record your findings by listing the activities of the children under the appropriate motor task. You can use as examples activities that were planned by the teachers or those that were spontaneously a part of the children's play.

Using ideas from your observations, develop a week's plan for physical development activities. Be sure to include all of the eight categories of perceptual-motor activities and plan at least two activities in each category during that week. Try to think of interesting possibilities that the children would enjoy. After your plan is complete, evaluate the results.

1. Are all the categories covered with appropriate activities at least twice during the week?

2. Are all the activities safe?

3. Will they provide enough range of difficulty so that more and less skilled children are attracted to them and can participate?

references for further reading

Greenman, J. (1998). *Caring Spaces, Learning Places: Children's Environments That Work.* Redmond, WA: Exchange Press.

Miller, K. (1989). *The Outside Play and Learning Book: Activities for Young Children.* Mt. Rainier, MD: Gryphon House.

Sanders, S.W., & Youngue, B. (1998). Challenging Movement Experiences for Young Children. *Dimensions of Early Childhood* 26(1), 9-17.

Torbert, M., & Schneider, M.A. (1993). *Follow Me Too: A Handbook of Movement Activities for Three- to Five-Year-Olds.* Menlo Park, CA: Addison-Wesley.

notes

unit 3
infants in group care

video program: *babies are children, too*

caring for infants and toddlers in group settings

unit overview

Read this section before reading the text assignment.

The topic of infants and toddlers in out-of-home group care is becoming increasingly important as more of our youngest children spend their early years in child care programs. This chapter is intended to help beginning caregivers "get their bearings" when working with children under the age of 3. Students will learn the importance of providing high-quality care and the essential principles in so doing.

unit objectives

Read these objectives before reading the text assignment.

THIS UNIT:

1. Helps you understand the value of providing high-quality care for infants and toddlers.

2. Defines the essential components of high-quality care for infants and toddlers.

3. Acquaints you with the basics of infant development and developmentally appropriate practices.

4. Provides strategies for responding to special issues in the first three years, such as: crying and communication with infants, separation and stranger anxiety, the development of autonomy, tantrums and toilet training.

5. Suggests that students who work with infants make a professional commitment and advocate for high quality and an upgrading of the profession.

text assignment

Read this assignment, which is found in this guide immediately following the student activities and references (pp. 35-67).

Unit 3, "Caring for Infants and Toddlers in Group Settings," *The Whole Child Student Guide*, Patricia Weissman.

focus for learning

It is important to realize that working with infants and toddlers is a unique experience which is quite different from working with older children. It takes special skills, teaching strategies and commitment in order to provide high-quality care, as opposed to "babysitting." High-quality programs for infants are very important as these early years are crucial ones in the child's development.

The video program, *Babies are Children Too,* can be a valuable tool in promoting thought and stimulating ideas for role-playing and practical experience. Use the following section of **Video-Related Questions** to help you begin to think about some of the important issues that the video program will address. That way, when similar questions are posed in the video, you can begin to think about what your responses might be. Being an active viewer of the video program will help you to respond to the following **Video-Related Questions for Reflection and Role Play** in a more meaningful way.

video-related questions for reflection and role play

Read these questions before viewing the video program. After viewing the program, respond to all these questions by interacting with another person, aloud to yourself or in your journal. Try to find opportunities to role play or practice the approaches illustrated.

1. Why are consistent, long-term relationships so important to an infant's development?

2. How is working with infants and toddlers different from working with older children? What are some of the special skills an infant/toddler caregiver would need to have in order to provide good care?

3. What temperamental styles have you seen in babies? How do you think you should respond to babies with different temperamental styles? Role play how you would respond on an individual basis to babies with different temperamental styles, such as: a quiet, fearful infant; a boisterous, more demanding baby; and one who is flexible and happy-go-lucky.

4. What did you observe during the diaper changing scene in the video tape? How was communication between the caregiver and child maximized? How do you think diaper changing should be handled?

5. Why is hand washing in infant and toddler centers so important? When and how should hand washing be done and by whom? Discuss universal precautions and health standards for diapering and toileting.

6. What are some of your ideas for keeping infants and toddlers healthy and safe? What steps would you take to reduce illness among infants in group care? What steps would you take to provide a safe indoor and outdoor environment for infants and toddlers?

7. Why are relationships and communication with families especially important when working with infants? What ideas do you have for maximizing communication with families?

8. How do you think infants and toddlers with special needs can be integrated into child care programs? Discuss the impact of the IDEA act on child care programs.

9. How do you feel about talking to babies? What ideas do you have for supporting infant and toddler language development? How would you handle families that speak a different language from their own?

10. How would you handle tantrums or other examples of toddlers asserting themselves? What do you think about "time out"? Think of other means for setting clear, developmentally-appropriate limits without using time out for toddlers. Try to role play situations where you are setting limits for an uncooperative toddler.

predicaments for your consideration

Respond to these predicaments with another person, aloud to yourself or in your journal.

1. You are an infant caregiver in a small child care center or family child care home. A 9 month-old baby has just been enrolled in your program. After meeting with the parents, you've found out that the infant tends to cry inconsolably whenever her parents leave the room. In addition, the child has never been left with another caregiver for more than an hour or two. What steps would you take to ease the transition to full-time, out-of-home care? Explain why. Describe some of the discussion you would like to have with the parents and suggestions you might make.

2. A family in your center has informed you that it is their cultural practice to begin toilet training when the child turns one year old. How would you handle this situation? What are your beliefs about how to go about toilet training and why?

assignment for students working or volunteering with infants and toddlers

Complete this assignment and submit the written response to your instructor.

Spend some time observing the children in your care and then provide a detailed account that includes the following:

1. each child's age

2. a description of each child's temperamental pattern with some examples

3. a description of each child's developmental abilities with some examples

Look over your descriptions. In what way is each baby unique? In which ways are these children alike? Based on this information, how do you think you can support each child's development?

observational assignment

Complete this assignment and submit the written response to your instructor.

Try to observe in an infant/toddler center or family child care home for a whole morning or afternoon. Take notes and then write a summary of the following:

Analyze the following statement with regard to your observations: "For infant and toddler caregivers, the single most important goal is to establish warm, caring, attentive relationships with each individual child."

What were the indications that the caregiver established caring relationships with each child? How did the infants and toddlers express their needs and desires? How did the caregiver respond? What sorts of interactions and communication took place between the teacher and each child? What recommendations would you make, if any, for strengthening the relationships between the caregiver and each child?

references for further reading

Anderson, P.O. & Fenichel, E.S. (1989). *Serving culturally diverse families of infants and toddlers with disabilities.* Arlington, VA: ZERO TO THREE.

Gonzalez-Mena, J. & Eyer, D.W. (1989). *Infants, toddlers and caregivers.* Mountain View, CA: Mayfield.

Honig, A.S. (1985). High quality infant/toddler care. *Young children,* 41 (1).

Lally, J.R., et al. (1995). *Caring for infants and toddlers in groups: Developmentally appropriate practice.* Arlington, VA: ZERO TO THREE.

caring for infants and toddlers in group setttings

by
Patricia Weissman, Ed.D
The Merrill-Palmer Institute
Wayne State University

"Babies and children, by their inborn nature keep reaching out to people and things. Fond parents, watching and coaxing, respond enthusiastically to their baby's first smiles with smiles of their own, head noddings and declarations of love. Repetitions of this scene, every waking hour for months, along with hugs, comforting during misery, and the offering of food at times of hunger keep reinforcing feelings of love and trust. These form the foundation on which the child's future relationships with all the other people in her life will be built. Even her interest in things, and her later capacity to deal with ideas and concepts, in school and occupation, will depend on this foundation of love and trust."

– Benjamin Spock and Michael Rothenberg. *Baby and Child Care.* New York: E. P. Dutton, Inc. 1985.

"In response to a growing need for alternative care for infants and toddlers, the number of group infant care programs in the United States has been increasing steadily, and this trend will probably continue. It is no longer appropriate to ask whether children should be placed in child care or be cared for at home . . . what is needed is information for families about what to look for in obtaining high quality care. Caregivers are also seeking guidance about how to provide the best care for infants and toddlers."

– Victoria Fu. Infant Toddler Care in Centers. In Dittman, L. (Ed.) *The Infants We Care For.* Washington, D.C.: National Association for the Education of Young Children. 1984.

Have you ever . . .

Wondered what there is to do all day with a group of babies?

Wanted to know what to do when an infant cries after being left by his parent?

Wondered what to do in the face of a *magnificent* toddler tantrum?

If you have, the material in the following pages will help you.

Infancy is a unique and amazing time of life. Those who work as infant and toddler caregivers are able to enjoy the rapid growth that occurs during the child's earliest years and form deep, affectionate bonds with each child. But often, caring for infants in a group setting can be extremely demanding and difficult. Even caregivers with the best intentions are sometimes left wondering if they've done the right thing. And despite the growing need for early child care, few states require any training in handling infants, so many teachers find themselves ill-prepared for the special challenges that arise when taking care of a group of babies or toddlers (Children's Defense Fund, 1989).

This chapter is intended to help those who are beginning to work with infants and toddlers to "get their bearings." It is impossible to cover all the important topics related to infancy in one chapter and it is highly recommended that caregivers seek out the additional resources listed at the back of the chapter.

a note about terminology

Throughout this chapter the term "infant" or "baby" refers to children around one year of age or younger, while "toddler" refers to children roughly between the ages of 16 and 36 months. Because child care for infants and toddlers involves both education and caring, the terms "teacher" and "caregiver" are used interchangeably. As the overwhelming majority of infant and toddler caregivers are women, teachers will be referred to as "she," whereas the use of "he" and "she" will be alternated when referring to children.

growing need for infant and toddler programs

The demand for programs for our youngest children started in the 1970s when most mothers with children under 3 years began working outside the home. More than 20 years later, the United States is still experiencing a major shift in how young children are being reared. In 1993, 59 percent of all women with preschoolers were in the work force, representing a five-fold increase from 11 percent in 1948. Currently, there are roughly 15 million infants and toddlers whose parents are in the labor force, with about half of these children being cared for in out-of-home group programs (Cost, Quality & Outcomes Study Team, 1995).

Research has shown that infants can and do thrive in out-of-home care when the quality of the care is good (Galinsky, et al., 1994, Howes, et al., 1995, Howes, et al., 1992, NICHD, 1996, Philips and Howes, 1987, Whitebook, et al., 1990). Yet, high-quality infant programs have not kept up with the demand. According to a national study, 40 percent of the infant centers examined were of such poor quality to be "possibly injurious." Problems cited in the study included safety and health hazards, lack of toys and unresponsive caregivers (Ibid.). In addition, a study of family child care (the most prevalent form of infant care), found that only 9 percent of the family daycare homes were rated as good quality, 56 percent were adequate or custodial, and 35 percent were rated as inadequate or growth-harming (Galinsky, et al., 1994). These studies point out the need for providing high quality care for infants and toddlers in group programs. Teacher preparation programs such as the Child Development Associate (CDA) credential and accreditation for child care centers through the National Association for the Education of Young Children (NAEYC) are initiatives designed to help upgrade the early childhood profession and in fact, NAEYC-accredited programs have been found to provide higher quality care (National Center for the Early Childhood Workforce, 1997).

Over the past few years there has been increasing concern about the problems of children from newborn to the age of three. The White House Conference on Early Child Development and Learning, held in 1997, focused attention on what was identified as a "quiet crisis" in the lives of our youngest children. The recent neuroscience research that was reported at the conference indicates that the first 3 years of life are critical for developing brain structures and that good early care is crucial in realizing a child's potential (DiCresce, 1997 and Newberger, 1997). The most notable federal initiative, Early Head Start, was created in the mid-nineties to provide a variety of services to "at-risk" families with children under the age of 3, based on the premise that intervention is necessary in the very earliest years. We can expect more programs and services for our youngest children as awareness about the importance of the first three years continues to grow.

types of programs

Family Child Care

Family child care is the primary source of infant and toddler care in this country – in fact there are more infants and toddlers in family daycare homes than there are those being cared for by their parent at home (Galinsky, et al., 1994). Family child care or family daycare homes refer to care for a small group of children in the provider's own home. Some family daycare homes are licensed by a state agency, though most are unlicensed (Ibid.). Licensing regulations vary from state to state, with adult to infant ratios ranging from one adult to every three infants, to one adult to every seven infants. The total number of children that a caregiver may take in the home also varies according to state, usually between six and 12 children (Kontos, 1992).

Some of the benefits of family child care are: the intimate, home-like atmosphere that often exists when a caregiver takes children into her own home, and the ability to form deep, caring relationships with each child and family.

Center-Based Care

Center-based care or child care centers are facilities outside the home, in a school site, business-zoned building, church facility or on-site at a corporation. Most child care centers are licensed, with stricter guidelines and procedures than family child care.[1] As with family child care, regulations for licensing vary widely from state to state. Center-based care is the least prevalent form of infant and toddler care, with 19 percent of 2 year olds and seven percent of infants under the age of one year enrolled in child care centers (U.S. Department of Education, 1995). Many child care centers serve only preschoolers, although the number of centers taking in infants and toddlers is increasing to meet the growing demand.

Some of the benefits of center-based care are: closer adherence to licensing standards such as health, safety and fire requirements; many center-based teachers are required to have more training and experience than those in family child care; and centers are able to apply for accreditation through the National Association for the Education of Young Children, which is associated with higher quality care (National Center for the Early Childhood Work Force, 1997).

---

[1] Stricter adherence to licensing guidelines, however, does not ensure higher quality. Studies of center-based infant care have shown most to be of mediocre or poor quality (Cost, Quality & Outcomes Study Team, 1995).

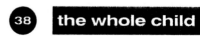

issues of quality in infant and toddler care

Given that most of our nation's infants and toddlers are in out-of-home care, it is important to consider the quality of care they are receiving. After all, more growth and development occurs during the first three years of life than any other time throughout the human lifespan, particularly with regard to brain development (DiCresce, 1997 and Newberger, 1997).

> Human infants usually come into the world with a well-organized capacity for adapting to their environment. Much of this capacity is attributable to our unique central nervous system. But the unfolding of the developing brain is not inevitable. It depends on a fostering environment, one that is reasonably stable while at the same time stimulating, responsive, protective and loving. When nurturing conditions are absent, the baby becomes apathetic and loses weight. Pediatricians refer to this as 'failure to thrive.' This condition is easy to recognize, but less extreme forms of environmental deficiency can have negative effects that may go unnoticed but that may nevertheless threaten the child's future (The Carnegie Corporation Task Force on Meeting the Needs of Young Children, 1994).

Certainly, none of us wishes to leave a detrimental and lasting impact on the developing infant. The rest of this chapter will help caregivers determine what can be done to provide a high-quality program for groups of infants and toddlers.

suggestions for providing high-quality infant and toddler care

There are several factors to keep in mind to ensure high-quality child care for infants and toddlers. The following list of suggestions is by no means exhaustive, but represents the most important components to include in order to help our youngest children off to a good start.

Goal 1: Focus on Relationships

For infant and toddler caregivers, the single most important goal is to establish warm, caring, attentive relationships with each individual child. Research has shown that the quality of the relationship between the caregiver and child is central to providing high-quality care that enhances development (Galinsky, et al., 1994, Howes, et al., 1995, NICHD, 1996, and Philips and Howes, 1987).

When a caregiver responds to a baby in a sensitive and consistent manner, the child develops a sense of security, a feeling that someone in the world is paying attention and will take care of her. As these appropriate and caring responses continue over time, the child forms an attachment with the caregiver. This attachment provides a secure base which the infant uses as a springboard for explorations of the physical, sensory and social world around her (Raikes, 1996, and Ainsworth, et al., 1978). Experienced infant and toddler teachers are familiar with the way in which a securely attached child will cuddle and play for awhile with the adult and then crawl or toddle off to explore another part of the room, occasionally looking back to the caregiver. Without a sense of security and trust, an infant seems to feel too fearful for independent exploration and learning (Erikson, 1950, and Ainsworth, et al., 1978).

Infants who are securely attached to their caregivers tend to grow up with many advantages over those who do not form secure attachments. Secure attachments foster competency in language, cognitive, social and emotional development (Leiberman, 1977, Matas, et al., 1978, Main and Weston, 1981). Studies of group infant care indicate that babies who are securely attached to a teacher tend to explore more, play better and have more social interactions than do babies whose caregivers are ever-changing or emotionally distant (Raikes, 1996).

Goal 2: Become an Engaged Caregiver

Engaged caregiving or "involved teaching" (Howes, et al., 1992) is the polar opposite of routine caretaking or "babysitting." In a study of center-based infant care, involved teachers were found to engage in more touching, hugging, holding, prolonged conversation and interactive joy. In addition, it was found that the babies who had involved teachers tended to be more securely attached to their teachers (Ibid.).

An engaged caregiver spends time carefully observing the infants and toddlers in her care to determine how each child communicates, reacts to others and responds to stimulation. Based upon these observations, the caregiver can then meet the child's needs in a way that is responsive to that particular baby or toddler. An engaged caregiver can usually tell when a child is coming down with a cold or teething, whether he needs a hug or a diaper change. An engaged caregiver is usually available to the children in a physical sense as well, often sitting on the floor with the babies and providing much-needed comfort such as hugging, cuddling, holding and lap sitting.

Goal 3: Use Daily Caregiving Routines as a Source of Engagement

Daily routines, such as feeding, napping, diapering, toileting and handwashing, offer rich opportunities for interaction between the teacher and child. These caregiving tasks should not be rushed through in an impersonal manner, rather, they can be used as a pleasant time for social contact and conversation. A caregiver who talks, plays, maintains eye contact and smiles during diaper changing (when culturally appropriate), indicates to the child that her needs will be met in a caring and responsive way. A teacher who holds and rocks a baby before putting him in the crib, helps him feel secure in the knowledge that he is well cared for and valued. And a caregiver who holds each baby during bottle-feeding — never leaving a baby alone with a propped-up bottle! – is responding to one of the most basic infant needs, that of close physical contact with a comforting adult.

This type of engagement cannot be accomplished through strict scheduling. Therefore, it is very important that caregivers try to be flexible in meeting infants' needs. Infants should be fed, napped and changed *as needed*, not as dictated by a schedule. Of course, this is where the "art" of infant caregiving becomes most apparent: what happens if three babies need diaper changes at the same time? Experienced caregivers find that as they observe and get to know each baby, a rhythm or pattern emerges. Usually a sensitive teacher is able to tell through nonverbal cues when each child in her care will get sleepy or hungry or need changing. Balancing the needs of infants and toddlers is not an easy task and it requires careful observation, sensitive responsiveness and flexible planning.

Goal 4: Build Strong Relationships with Each Family

Building strong relationships with each child's family is especially important during the child's first three years. When parents leave their baby in child care, they are taking a big leap of faith: they are trusting the caregiver to love and take good care of their child. Additionally, new parents often experience intense feelings of grief and guilt when they first leave their baby with another person, especially someone they don't know well. *Open, on-going communication with infant and toddler parents is essential.*

Families need to know that their baby is in good hands. Many infant caregivers find it useful to keep notes throughout the day which record such things as feeding times and what was eaten, diaper changes, bottles and medicines given. In addition, we need information from the child's family on a daily basis: How did she sleep last night? Is she getting a new tooth or is she ready to try a new food? This sort of communication should be built into infant and toddler programs so that it occurs naturally every day. Brief written notes about something the child did that day, telephone calls, casual conversation and scheduled meetings all contribute to effective communication with families.

Let's remember that family members know their children best so our aim is to work in partnership with families to determine the optimal course. Childrearing beliefs are very personal and deeply held; it is vital that we respect each family's beliefs and practices, and discuss differences openly. Our role as teachers extends to families as well, and we can advocate for developmentally appropriate practice in our programs by keeping parents informed about child development and the methods we use.

Goal 5: Provide Nonsexist Infant and Toddler Care

One of the most important developments during the first three years is the child's concept of self. Part of self-concept is gender identity – a sense of who we are and how to behave based on our identity as a male or female. Most young children are aware very early on whether they are a boy or a girl and their feelings about their gender influence how they perceive themselves (Gonzalez-Mena and Eyer, 1989).

Children can grow up with a severely limited view of their capabilities and potentials by being taught narrow sex roles. When working with infants and toddlers, let's try to offer each child a full range of possibilities, activities and expectations. Pay close attention to the types of comments we make to our babies, avoiding stereotypical terms such as "sweet, little girl" and "he's a bruiser" and instead focusing our attention on more meaningful observations such as "You're trying so hard to pull yourself up. What a strong baby you are!" or "What a sweet smile you're giving me!"

Also be sure to have plenty of books on hand that portray girls and boys in an egalitarian, nonsexist light. Boy and girl babies and toddlers should have equal access to materials that offer a wide range of activity – from fine motor manipulation such as reaching, grabbing objects and nesting to large motor activities that encourage crawling, rolling and scooting. Encourage boys and girls equally to explore, try out new things and experience all aspects of the development of the *whole* child.

We should pay attention to the messages we send out when dealing with adults, as well. Let's make men feel welcome and valued in our infant programs. Be sure to maintain communication and eye contact with fathers *and* mothers – avoid directing all questions and concerns to the mother. Ask fathers questions about the infant's caregiving needs and pass the baby to him at pick-up time, too. Let's also encourage men to engage in infant and toddler caregiving tasks and serve as models for our youngest children by hiring men in infant programs and asking fathers to volunteer whenever possible.

Goal 6: Promote Culturally Appropriate Practice for Infants and Toddlers

Cultural diversity has increased dramatically in this country. Over the past 15 years, the Asian/Pacific Islander population in the United States has increased more than 100 percent and the Hispanic population more than 50 percent (Rothlein and Meinbach, 1996). Infant and toddler teachers often work with families from diverse backgrounds and we can expect these cross-cultural interactions to continue (Aldridge and Booker, 1996).

The culture we come from influences our behavior and attitudes throughout our lives. How close we stand to people, whether we make eye contact, what gestures we make, the foods we eat and how we talk, are all influenced by our culture. Additionally, each of us develops attitudes about children and their expected behavior from within our cultural environment, and these attitudes underlie our caregiving practices (Gonzalez-Mena and Eyer, 1989). Each of us has a feeling about what is "normal" and "right" with regard to taking care of babies and toddlers. The first step in promoting culturally appropriate practice involves examining our own beliefs and attitudes toward young children.

Cultural identity is a part of the child's developing self-concept. It is important that we make every effort to find out about each child's family and cultural heritage in order to support a positive self-concept. We can observe how parents interact with their infants and toddlers and honor their method of communication. We can use outside resources to find out as much as possible about the family's culture without making generalizations. Let's encourage parents to share their language and customs at the center and adjust our interactions with children to honor and respect their cultures. Some cultures, for example, avoid celebrating birthdays or national holidays (Aldridge and Booker, 1996). In addition, we can seek out resources and materials, such as books, pictures, multi-hued paints and dolls that reflect the infant's race and culture.

Goal 7: Show Respect for Infants and Toddlers

Many adults pick babies up, carry them around, strap them in a highchair, or begin feeding them without ever saying a word to the child. Many teachers tell toddlers to "stop crying, you're okay," or try to distract an upset baby by giving him a bottle. Many infant caregivers will talk about a baby – even say negative things like, "she is such a cry-baby!" right in front of the child, assuming it's all over her head. These common practices are disrespectful and diminish the child's autonomy and sense of self.

Infants come into this world full of potential and strengths. Recent research has highlighted early infant abilities. For example, we now know that learning occurs within the first hours after birth and even within the womb, and that infants are "wired" from the start for social interaction and communication (DiCresce, 1997, and Newberger, 1997). The old notion of the infant as a "blank slate" has been erased, and instead we now see babies as active learners from the start. Infant and toddler teachers can benefit their children by respecting each individual child's set of inner resources, interests, personality and developmental pattern. We can do this primarily in two ways:

1. Discover and respect each baby's personality and temperament.

2. Discover and respect each baby's pattern of development.

Each baby is unique. Each baby has her own preferences, interests and responses to people and the world around her. Respecting an infant means appreciating who she is as an individual. A respectful caregiver will come to know each child in her care in a deep and intimate way, understanding what constitutes too much stimulation for a particular baby, what frightens him, what makes him smile. A respectful caregiver understands that each baby comes equipped with a personality or temperamental style. Infant researchers have identified three basic temperamental patterns:

*   The "flexible" child who is generally open to new people and experiences, is not alarmed by sudden occurrences and adapts quickly to what is going on.

*   The "feisty" child who is energetic, active and can seem more demanding.

*   The "fearful" child who appears shy and easily alarmed. These children like to take their time in approaching new people, activities or objects.

    (Lally, et al., 1995, and Thomas and Chess, 1977).

Not all babies can be expected to be outgoing and affectionate, cheerful and easy all the time like those we see in commercials. Some babies are quiet and shy. Some are easily frustrated. Some cry a lot. A respectful caregiver will vary her responses based on each baby's temperamental pattern and personality.

Each baby's pattern of development is unique as well. Although it is important to understand what constitutes typical or normal development (see Appendix A, Chart of Developmental Milestones), we should keep in mind that these developmental norms indicate a *range* of behaviors that occur at *varying times for different children.* These charts simply provide a general time frame for typical development and it is not expected that every child will perform every task at the same age. Let's allow each child in our care to develop at her own rate, without undue emphasis on whether she is "gifted" or "slow." Our goal should never be to push or speed up development, but rather to enhance it through good quality interactions and experiences.

Goal 8: Keep the Child to Adult Ratio Low; Keep the Total Group Size Small

In order for warm and nurturing relationships to develop between the caregiver and child, the adult cannot be responsible for a large number of children. Studies have consistently shown that high-quality child care is associated with fewer infants and toddlers per teacher and fewer children in the total group (National Center for the Early Childhood Work Force, 1997; Cost, Quality & Outcomes Study Team, 1995; Galinsky, et al., 1994).

To provide optimal care it is recommended that the maximum group size for infants is six, with each adult caring for no more than three babies and the maximum group size for toddlers is twelve, with each adult caring for no more than six toddlers – preferably four for young toddlers (Bredekamp and Copple, editors, 1997; Lally, et al., 1995). Because relationships are so important during these first years, it is also recommended that within each group, "primary caregiving groups" are formed where each child has a primary caregiver – one assigned adult – whom the infant can rely on to consistently meet his needs:

> Primary caregiving means that the infant or toddler and his family have someone special with whom to build an intimate relationship. A policy of primary caregiver assignments is strong evidence that a child care program takes seriously the importance of continuing, positive, intimate relationships. Primary caregiving is essential to

a child care program philosophy that values relationships. It is a statement to families that relationships are the key to quality caregiving (Lally, et al., 1995).

Goal 9: Promote Health and Safety

Despite our best efforts, young children in group care tend to get sick a lot. For one thing, their immunities to infectious diseases are just beginning to build. Also, they are in close, intimate contact with a number of other children and adults – all of whom pass on germs.

However, there are several precautions we can take that will significantly reduce the amount of contagious illness in our infant programs. The single most effective way to reduce illness in child care is simple: handwashing, *lots* of handwashing. More germs are spread during the course of the day through contact from hands than any other source, including sneezing or coughing. It is important that caregivers wash their own hands:

- upon arrival
- before preparing food, eating or feeding a child
- after toileting self or a child
- after changing a diaper
- after wiping a runny nose

It is important to wash infants' hands, as well, holding them at the sink or using disposable wipes. When children are able to wash their own hands, we should teach them how to do a thorough job, always using liquid soap, and supervise them until they are consistent in doing so (NAEYC, 1995).

Additional measures we should take to reduce illness include:

1. Wear disposable gloves for diaper changing and dispose of gloves after each change. Disinfect the changing area after each use with a bleach solution made daily (1 tablespoon of bleach to 1 quart of water).

2. Make sure the areas for food preparation and diapering are separate.

3. Disinfect toys and surfaces on a daily basis; disinfect all toys that have been mouthed by a baby before another child uses them.

4. Establish a clear illness policy for families and staff which excludes contagious children – and adults – from group care.

5. Work with families to ensure medical care and immunizations are updated.

6. Make sure.all caregivers are trained in pediatric first aid and emergency breathing techniques.

7. As a precaution against Sudden Infant Death Syndrome, the American Academy of Pediatrics recommends placing infants on their backs for napping. Pillows should not be used, and soft materials like blankets and stuffed animals should be kept to a minimum.

Safety is another important issue we must address in group programs for infants and toddlers. Babies and toddlers learn through moving their bodies and exploring their surroundings. As infants develop and begin to crawl and then walk, they seem to "get into everything" in an attempt to explore the world around them. Teachers must supervise infants and toddlers at all times. This means being able to see and hear them – even at naptime – to make sure they are out of harm's way. We should also make indoor and outdoor safety checks on a daily basis to make sure electrical outlets are covered, there are no objects around that a child could choke on, equipment is undamaged, etc. It is helpful to look at our rooms and playground from a toddler's eye view: what looks enticing? What could be dismantled or broken? What might be attractive to put into the mouth?

Goal 10: Provide an Enriching and Developmentally Appropriate Environment

The spaces we use for infant and toddler programs should be carefully planned and continually evaluated to make sure we are providing an enriching and appropriate environment. Young babies need many opportunities for exploration of their senses and moving bodies. Babies should have plenty of interesting objects and mobiles around to look at and reach for. The environment should be well-organized and clutter-free, where objects are placed on low shelves or in bins. Our rooms should offer many curiosities and challenging choices that encourage looking, touching, moving and exploring the world at the infant's own pace. However, these challenges should not be overwhelming to the child. Too much stimulation (constant loud noise, overly bright lights and colors, too many children or objects, etc.) will create an environment that is stressful and uncomfortable for the child.

Babies and toddlers like to explore other people, too. Let's provide adequate, comfortable space in which children can crawl, cuddle, hug, sit beside and interact with others. Let's make sure there are places where babies can be with others in a small group and places where a baby can curl up in privacy or with a caregiver. Big, soft pillows on the floor and low couches will encourage caregivers to stay at "baby-level" and be available for lap-sitting, cuddling or reading.

Comfort and efficiency should also be considered when arranging child care spaces. Infants and toddlers need a separate nap room that is relaxing, quiet and soothing. There should be separate areas for feeding and diapering, as well. Convenient storage areas are very important, as are comfortable spaces for parents to visit, talk with the children and caregivers, and store their child's belongings.

Goal 11: Develop a Program that is Inclusive of Children with Special Needs

Of the nearly 3.7 million children born each year in the United States, approximately 55,000 infants will manifest a disabling condition at birth, with another 370,000 children developing a disabling condition during the first 4 years (Garwood, et al., 1988). With the creation in 1986 of the Education of the Handicapped Amendments Act– Part C (now called the Individuals with Disabilities Education Act or IDEA), states are now required to provide services to infants and toddlers with handicaps and their families. For many children with special needs, this means their inclusion in child care centers and family daycare homes. Infant and toddler teachers should become familiar with common disabilities and methods for integrating children with special needs into child care programs (see Chapter 9 of *The Whole Child*).

The integration of most infants and toddlers with mild handicapping conditions requires very little adaptation of the child care program. What we already know to be the best practice for infants and toddlers is also the best practice for children with special needs (Sexton, 1990). To a large extent, the successful integration of infants and toddlers with handicaps requires a responsive and engaged caregiver. Successful integration of children with special needs also requires that caregivers make communication with the child's family a top priority. Parents are the most valuable resource teachers have in meeting the needs of exceptional children because they know their children best.

Exceptional infants and toddlers should be encouraged to participate in usual activities in the center with modifications provided only when necessary to ensure success. We should encourage independence without demanding skills that lie beyond the child's ability, and we should be careful not to pity or overprotect babies with special needs. Acceptance of the child's limitations as well as capitalization on her strengths is the balance to strive for and to model for the family.

Goal 12: Make a Commitment to Professionalism

As the need for infant and toddler care continues to grow, more teachers find themselves working with our very youngest children. Infant caregiving requires a special kind of person, not everyone feels comfortable developing the warm, intimate relationships that infants and toddlers require. But because child care is a relatively easy field of employment for anyone to enter, and because it requires relatively little training to work in child care, many harmful practices have become common occurrences in the lives of young children.

We now understand the importance of the first three years of life. Those of us who work with infants and toddlers bear the responsibility of providing a high quality, nurturing experience during these formative years. Part of this responsibility means being committed to providing the best for our children *over the long run.* Infants and toddlers do not fare well when their caregivers leave. Infants and toddlers need a long time with a consistent, caring adult for their development to blossom. Unfortunately, child care programs experience extremely high levels of turnover – more than twice the national average for other fields of employment (Whitebook, et al., 1993).

Much of the problem stems from low wages and lack of benefits. Most teachers in child care centers earn less than $7 an hour and receive no medical insurance (Whitebook, et al., 1993 and Child Outcomes Study Team, 1995) and family child care providers earn even less (Galinsky, et al., 1994). In studies of child care center quality, the number one predictor of high quality was higher staff salaries (Whitebook, et al., 1993).

If we are committed to providing the best for our youngest children, then we must advocate for massive changes in our early care system. We can talk with parents, educate our communities and become politically active in advocating for respect and decent wages for the important work of infant caregiving.

special considerations for infant and toddler teachers

Because working with infants and toddlers is so different from teaching older children, I've included some issues to think about that probably confront every infant and toddler caregiver. Those who work with our youngest children should be prepared to deal with such issues as crying, separation anxiety, stranger anxiety, discipline, tantrums and toilet learning in a calm, professional and growth-enhancing way. It is important to understand the developmental nature of these potentially stressful issues and to have an appropriate plan of action in mind.

Crying

Those of us who work with groups of young infants have probably all felt the stress that comes when two or three babies begin crying, loudly and intensely, at the same time. There is no other sound that can cause such immediate and extreme feelings of discomfort in adults as a baby —or worse, a group of babies— crying.

Let's keep in mind that babies do not cry to upset us. Crying is one of the main resources infants possess for communicating their needs, desires and thoughts. Young babies cry to tell us that they are hungry or tired, that they have gas pain, or just want to be held. Some infants seem to cry simply to exercise their lungs; some infants just *need* to cry during certain times of the day and will do so, like clockwork, for perhaps an entire hour. Many babies cannot fall asleep until they have experienced the relief that comes from a good, hard cry.

Our goal as infant caregivers should not be to extinguish all crying in our group programs. Babies have the need and the *right* to cry. However, this doesn't mean we should ever ignore our children's crying. By developing close relationships with the infants in our care and carefully observing their communication patterns, we can try to learn what each baby's cries mean. After all, not all cries are the same: a baby's cry of pain will sound very different from her cry at being overly tired. And just as the baby's cries are different, so our responses should be, too. When we respond promptly and with appropriate comfort, we communicate back to the child that someone is out there to care for her.

Here are a few tips for dealing with crying in group infant care:

- Always listen and observe when a baby is crying and try to figure out why.

- Respond quickly and appropriately to a baby's cries, as best you can. If he is hungry, feed him, if he wants to be held, pick him up.

- Sometimes, in group care, we can't respond quickly enough to each baby's cries. Set your priorities: Which baby needs comfort first? When you can't respond immediately to a baby, talk to her, as your voice is a source of comfort as well.

- Babies cry to communicate and babies just need to cry sometimes. Responding to a baby's cries will not result in "spoiling" the child, just as a crying baby is not a "bad" baby.

- Avoid trying to distract or lull crying babies by automatically giving them a pacifier or bottle or placing them in a wind-up swing.

- Maintain a calm, pleasant atmosphere so infants generally feel comfortable.

- Maintain warm, consistent relationships with each baby so all the infants in your care feel secure that their needs will be met.

Separation and Stranger Anxiety

Earlier in this chapter we learned about the process of attachment, when an infant forms an intense, loving bond with the adults who care for him. As infants develop these attachments with their family members and caregivers at the child care center, two related developments occur: a fear of separating from loved ones and a new fear of strangers. Both fears can be extremely distressing for the child; it is not uncommon for babies at this stage of development to become completely distraught and miserable when their parents or caregivers leave the room or scream in terror when a stranger approaches.

We should keep in mind that separation and stranger anxieties are healthy, normal developments that many babies experience during the second half of their first year. When babies develop these fears, it lets us know that they have formed healthy attachments with their caregivers and that they have the mental capacity to distinguish between loved ones and strangers. So despite the distress we experience when a baby shrieks and cries when being left, we should rest assured that this behavior usually indicates positive growth (Gonzalez-Mena and Eyer, 1989). But let's also keep in mind that each baby is unique and that's why it is so important to pay attention to each child's temperament, individual development, family and culture. Many infants who have healthy attachments do not show signs of separation anxiety or stranger anxiety. Parents of infants who go happily and easily to the caregiver at the center need not worry. Each baby is different: some babies exhibit extreme separation anxiety for a month while others have comparatively mild separation anxiety that lasts for six months. The way in which the baby is cared for can also affect the development of these anxieties. For example, in some cultures where babies have close associations with many different adults, they may not develop stranger anxiety and yet they still have healthy attachments with their caregivers.

Some suggestions for dealing with separation and stranger anxiety include:

- Try to avoid enrolling a new infant into a group program when she is at the peak of her anxiety. It is better to enroll the baby before anxiety sets in (in most cases, before six or seven months) or after the anxiety has lessened. It is beneficial to discuss with families their baby's level of separation anxiety before enrollment to determine the best time to start the child in group care.

- Communicate regularly with the child's family and reassure them that separation anxiety is not only typical, it usually indicates good, healthy development.

- Help families through the painful separations with their baby. Some parents have just as much trouble separating as their child — especially when they are left all day with the memory of their child's crying, distressed face. Encourage parents to telephone in a short while, but not to come back for additional good-byes once they have left. Reappearing after saying goodbye is not a comfort to the child and only prolongs his misery.

- Develop a ritual for separation with each family ("Okay, Daddy's going to go now. I'll be back later." Then a big hug and a kiss before handing the baby to the caregiver. Then the caregiver hugs and holds the child and goes to the window to wave good-bye.) By repeating this same scenario daily, the infant comes to understand that separation is a part of each day and that it is predicable and manageable.

- Use a special blanket, stuffed animal or other object from home as a "transitional object" to comfort the infant while separated from loved ones.

- Support the child's feelings and use soothing words to reassure her that her loved one will return. At the same time, avoid diminishing what the child is going through ("It's really not that bad.") or using bribes of food to lessen the child's feelings.

- Tell the baby with your words and behavior that you will take good care of him while his family is away or while in the presence of a stranger.

- Make sure your center is comfortable and comforting for infants, and that there are plenty of interesting activities and materials for the baby to engage in once she has calmed down.

Issues of Toddler Autonomy: Discipline, Tantrums, Toilet Learning

As children approach their second year, they begin to grow in independence and a sense of autonomy or self-governance (Erikson, 1950). Previously dependent behaviors from infancy are replaced by an urgent need to do it themselves. Taking off shoes, climbing up on a shelf to reach an object, pouring milk, putting on a jacket all become intensely important challenges for the toddler to assert his independence. When met with impatience and restrictions from the caregiver, a child in this stage of development will often collapse in tears or throw a tantrum.

The toddler can now assert herself through language, as well, and it is common to hear "No", "Mine!" and "Me do it!" frequently throughout the day. Although these behaviors can be very trying on adult caregivers, it is important to understand that they indicate positive and healthy development. Adults can assist toddlers in their quest for autonomy by responding in ways that support their needs to feel self-sufficient and capable. The challenge with toddlers is to find a balance between independence and setting necessary limits, between freedom and control. Toddlers need to do things themselves, but they also need the guidance and protection of a sensitive caregiver.

Discipline

Remember that the goal of discipline is not to punish, but to *teach* so that *self-discipline* can develop. Since we know that toddlers have an intense need to assert their independence, how can we discipline and guide them in a way that doesn't stifle their autonomy? Below are a few suggestions for avoiding punishment (which is relatively ineffective in teaching self-discipline) and instead helping toddlers learn to control their own behavior. Keep in mind that the development of self-discipline is a long process so be prepared to repeat many of these steps over and over. Be patient. Many toddler teachers say they prefer working with this age group because of the joy of seeing the individual strengths and personality of each child emerge so vibrantly as he develops his own sense of independence, self-discipline and self-worth.

The most effective discipline technique at our disposal is preventing problems before they happen. Since we know that toddlers need to feel capable and independent, let's offer them many opportunities for making responsible choices. For example, you can replace commands such as "It's time to sit down at the table," with a choice for the toddler to make: "Would you rather help set out napkins or plates?" The more a toddler feels powerful and in control of her choices, the less likely she is to assert her power in an undesirable way. Be creative. Think about your child care program and your children. How you can offer them plenty of opportunities to make appropriate choices throughout the day?

It is also important to provide toddlers with a variety of interesting developmentally appropriate activities and experiences so that they are actively engaged and less likely to cause provocation out of boredom. As we plan creative experiences for our toddlers, let's also incorporate as many choices for the child as possible, choices of colors, materials, what to make, where to go on a walk, and so on. And let's offer our toddlers many, many opportunities for feeling competent and masterful: have *them* make the play dough from scratch and commend them sincerely on their hard work.

Finally, we can help our toddlers avoid clashes by paying close attention to our environment, materials and program: Do certain areas of the room always seem to explode with conflict? Observe the environment and try to change "hot spots." Are there enough interesting materials to go around? Are certain items coveted and causing fights? Is our day's program over- or under-stimulating? Does each child feel like a valued and respected member of the group? Looking at our child care program through an autonomy-seeking toddler's eyes can help inform our daily practice and avoid many stressful situations.

However, even the best preventative measures cannot stop discipline problems from occurring altogether. What happens when a child refuses to stop pulling another's hair or simply will not put on her jacket before going out into the snow? Here are some suggestions for guidance and discipline with toddlers. Bear in mind, that there is not one perfect technique that will always work with all children. It is important to observe and try to understand each child's behavior and attempt solutions based upon your understanding of that particular child. And let's not forget how important it is to communicate with families and try to coordinate efforts to guide our toddlers toward self-control.

- Avoid power struggles with toddlers. Try to state limits in a positive way ("You can draw here on your paper.") rather than issuing a confrontational challenge ("Put that marker down right now!").

- Redirect undesirable behavior whenever possible. ("Let's sit over here and read a story. It's getting too wild at the sand table.")

- Stop aggressive or dangerous behavior. If a simple "no" and quick explanation works, fine; but if not you will need to provide physical control by stopping the child's hands or possibly removing him from the situation.

- Model the behavior you wish to see in the children. Avoid yelling, snapping at children or responding in anger. Sometimes it is helpful to take a pause, a few breaths, and then calmly maintain control. Remember that the toddler who is out of control is probably scared at being out of control and is relying on you for help and guidance.

- Help children cooperate with each other and try to solve their own problems by encouraging them to express their feelings with words. ("Tony, tell Rose how you felt when she took your crayon. Rose, use your words and ask Tony to pass you a crayon.")

- Avoid punishment or time-out with toddlers. Instead use this four-step plan for setting limits:

1. Explain the limit in a calm, simple way ("You cannot hit other children.").

2. Explain the reason for the limit ("Hitting hurts.").

3. Explain what the consequence will be if the child continues and make the consequence appropriate ("If you hit again you will have to leave the block area and come sit by me.").

4. Always follow through on the consequence.

- Be sure to pay attention to and comment favorably when you see positive behaviors –especially in children who are having many discipline struggles.

Tantrums

Toddlers have very intense feelings, desires and needs yet they are limited in their ability to express and fulfill them. The result is extreme frustration that is often released through a magnificent temper tantrum. During a tantrum, the child is out of control. This can be a very frightening experience for the child and he relies on his caregivers to help calm him and provide psychological security. This is why punishing a tantrum does no good, nor does attempting to talk and reason with the child. Although ignoring a tantrum is often the best policy, at no time should the child be out of an adult's sight.

Some guidelines for dealing with temper tantrums are:

- Calmly and carefully remove the child from the presence of other children. Find a quiet corner or, if there is adequate staffing and space, a separate room. Keep in mind that this is not a time-out.

- Reassure the other children who have witnessed the tantrum. Let them know the child is very upset and needs to be alone for a while but will come back when he is ready to play nicely.

- Stay near the child and tell her you will wait until she is ready to join the group again.

- Ignore the tantrum as much as possible, but when you see the child "winding down," make gentle invitations to join you in a calming activity. ("Would you like to sit on my lap for awhile now that you've calmed down?")

- Sometimes it is helpful to discuss what happened with the child. ("That was really scary. You seemed very angry and upset.") Sometimes it is best to just sit quietly and calmly together.

- When the child has regained control invite him to rejoin the group and help him enter back into the social realm. ("Are you ready to join the others now? I see Jamal is over at the water table. Would you like to join him?")

- Do not punish tantrums, but allow the child to experience natural consequences. ("It's too bad you were having that tantrum because now you've missed out on finger painting.")

Toilet Learning

Going to the toilet is a necessary social skill that most children develop sometime around their second year. The process of toilet learning takes time, understanding and patience. The most important rule is not to rush children into using the potty. As in all aspects of child care, communication with families is essential. The first step in the toilet learning process is talking with families about their ideas and beliefs. The more we can work in cooperation with families, the smoother toilet learning will be for the child.

There is no set age at which toilet learning should begin. The right time depends on each child's physical and emotional readiness. Between 18 and 24 months a child may have control over bladder and bowel movements, but many children are not ready until 30 months or older. Some children have no problem using the toilet regularly at the age of 2, while others don't achieve mastery until they are 3 or older (Black and Puckett, 1996). Indications that a child is ready to learn to use the toilet include:

- The child remains dry for at least 2 hours at a time or is dry after nap.
- The child indicates beforehand that a bowel movement or urination is about to occur.
- The child seems uncomfortable in wet or soiled diapers.
- The child asks to wear underwear.

Because toilet learning can be such a source of concern for parents, it is helpful to arrange a meeting for all the toddler families to discuss the issue. Have materials available for parents to read (see Recommended Resources at the end of this chapter) and perhaps a hand-out describing your approach. Toilet learning beliefs often reflect the family's culture and it is important to listen to each family's ideas. However, sometimes it is not possible to do exactly what each family prefers. In some cultures, children are *trained* very early by placing the child on the potty at very frequent intervals. Such a procedure would not be possible in a group care situation. For help in dealing with cultural issues during potty learning, I highly recommend *Multicultural Issues in Child Care* by Janet Gonzalez-Mena, who devotes a chapter to toilet training.

Here are some further ideas for encouraging healthy, respectful toilet learning in toddlers:

- Ask families to dress their child in clothing with elastic waistbands that the child can remove herself. Also, be sure there are plenty of extra clean clothes available for the child at the center.

- Keep the toileting experience positive and relaxed. Toilet learning is closely associated with how a child feels about himself and we never want to punish, humiliate or push children or compare their progress.

- When appropriate, toileting can be a pleasant group experience. When toddlers see their peers on a low potty, singing potty songs and enjoying the experience, they want to join in, too.

- Comment favorably when a child is successful and note how "grown-up" she is.

- Never display disappointment in a child who is not successful.

- Handle "accidents" in a calm, matter of fact manner and reassure the child that he has done nothing wrong.

- Careful sanitation procedures are a must. Each child's and adult's hands should be washed thoroughly after each attempt. Seats should be washed and disinfected with a bleach solution (1 tablespoon bleach to 1 quart water) after every single use.

summary

Providing high-quality care for infants and toddlers is not easy, yet many caregivers find it very rewarding to know we are setting off our youngest children on the right track. This chapter has suggested some basic goals to adopt to ensure that our infant and toddler care enhances children's development.

In summary, we have found that sustained, consistent and caring relationships between caregiver and child are critical. It is especially important that our group sizes remain small so we are available to satisfy each child's needs and engage in sensitive interactions. Routine caregiving tasks such as feeding, diaper changing and napping provide excellent opportunities for communication and interaction with each baby and toddler. Open communication and good rapport with families is especially important when working with our youngest children. High-quality infant and toddler programs are nonsexist and culturally appropriate, respecting each child's individuality and heritage. Infant and toddler teachers can help integrate children with special needs into child care programs. High-quality infant and toddler programs promote health and safety, and provide an environment that is stimulating but not overwhelming. And finally, infant and toddler teachers were encouraged to make a commitment to professionalism by staying with their children over a long period of time and by advocating for professional respect.

Those who work with our youngest children should be prepared to deal with such issues as crying, separation anxiety, stranger anxiety, discipline, tantrums and toilet learning in a calm, professional and growth-enhancing way. It is important to understand the developmental nature of these potentially stressful issues and to have an appropriate plan of action in mind.

The hallmarks of good infant and toddler care are really quite simple and basic. Our job is to help instill a sense of trust, safety and comfort in our children while responding with affection and respect to the needs and personalities of each individual child in our care. If we can do that, then we can leave work each day knowing that what we've given our infants and toddlers is a wonderful foundation and head start as they set out on their journey to becoming a whole child.

references

Aldridge, J., and Booker, B. (1996). Cultural diversity and early language and literacy development. *Association for Childhood Education International Infancy Division Newsletter,* 8 (4), 2-4.

Ainsworth, M. D. S., Blehar, M. C., Waters, E., and Wall, S. (1978). *Patterns of attachment: A psychological study of strange situations.* Hillsdale, NJ: Erlbaum.

Black, J. K., and Puckett, M. B. (1996). *The Young child: Development from prebirth through age eight.* Englewood Cliffs, NJ: Prentice-Hall.

Bredekamp, S., and Copple, C., (Eds.). (1997). *Developmentally appropriate practice in early childhood programs.* Washington, DC: National Association for the Education of Young Children.

Carnegie Corporation Task Force on Meeting the Needs of Young Children. (1994). *Starting points: Meeting the needs of our youngest children.* New York: Carnegie Corporation.

Children's Defense Fund. (1989). *A vision for America's future: An agenda for the 1990's: A children's defense budget.* Washington, DC: Author.

Cost, Quality & Outcomes Study Team. (1995). *Cost, quality and child outcomes in child care centers, technical report.* Denver: Department of Economics, University of Colorado.

DiCresce, A. (1997). Brain surges. *Wayne medicine.* Detroit: Wayne State University.

Erikson, E. (1950). *Childhood and society.* New York: Norton.

Fu, V. (1984). Infant toddler care in centers. In Dittman, L. (Ed.) *The infants we care for.* Washington, DC: National Association for the Education of Young Children.

Galinsky, E., Howes, C., Kontos, S., and Shinn, M. (1994). *The study of children in family child care and relative care: Highlights of findings.* New York: Families and Work Institute.

Garwood, S.G., Fewell, R. R., and Neisworth, J. T. (1988). Public law 94-142: You can get there from here! *Topics in early childhood special education,* 8, 1-11.

Gonzalez-Mena, J. (1993). *Multicultural issues in child care.* Mt. View, CA: Mayfield.

Gonzalez-Mena, J., and Eyer, D. W. (1989). *Infants, toddlers and caregivers.* Mt. View, CA: Mayfield.

Howes, C., Smith, E., and Galinsky, E. (1995). *The Florida child care quality improvement study: Interim report.* New York: Families and Work Institute.

Howes, C., Phillips, D. A., and Whitebook, M. (1992). Threshold of quality: Implications for the social development of children in center-based care. *Child development,* 63, 449-60.

Kontos, S. (1992). *Family day care: Out of the shadows and into the limelight.* Washington, DC: National Association for the Education of Young Children.

Lally, J. R., Griffin, A., Fenichel, E., Segal, M., Szanton, E., and Weissbourd, B. (1995). *Caring for infants and toddlers in groups: Developmentally appropriate practice.* Arlington, VA: ZERO TO THREE/The National Center.

Leiberman, A. (1977). Preschoolers competence with a peer: Relations with attachment and peer experience. *Child development,* 48, 1277-87.

Main, M., and Weston, D. (1981). The quality of toddler's relationships to mother and to father related to conflict behavior and readiness to establish new relationships. *Child development,* 52, 932-40.

Matas, L., Arend, R., and Sroufe, L. A. (1978). Continuity of adaptation in the second year: The relationship between quality of attachment and later competence. *Child development,* 49, 547-56.

National Center for the Early Childhood Workforce. (1997). *NAEYC accreditation as a strategy for improving child care quality.* Washington, DC: Author.

NAEYC. (1995). *Healthy young children: A manual for programs.* Washington, DC: National Association for the Education of Young Children.

NICHD Early Childhood Research Network, (1996). Characteristics of infant child care: Factors contributing to positive caregiving. *Early childhood research quarterly,* 11, 269-306.

Newberger, J. (1997). New brain development research—a wonderful window of opportunity to build public support for early childhood education! *Young children,* 52 (4), 4-9.

Philips, D. A., and Howes, C. (1987). Indicators of quality in child care: Review of the research. In Phillips, D. A. (Ed.). *Quality in child care: What does the research tell us?* Research Monograph of the National Association for the Education of Young Children, Vol.1. Washington, DC: NAEYC.

Raikes, H. (1996). A secure base for babies: Applying attachment concepts to the infant care setting. *Young children,* 51 (5), 59-67.

Rothlein, L., and Meinbach, A. (1996). *Legacies: Using children's literature in the classroom.* New York: HarperCollins.

Sexton, D. (1990). Quality, integrated programs for infants and toddlers with special needs. In Surbeck, E., and Kelley, M. (Eds.) *Personalizing care with infants, toddlers and families.* Wheaton, MD: Association for Childhood Education International.

Spock, B., and Rothenberg, M. (1985). *Baby and child care.* New York: E. P. Dutton.

Thomas, A., and Chess, S. (1977). *Temperament and development.* New York: Brunner/Mazel.

U.S. Department of Education. (1995). *National household education survey.* Washington, DC: National Center for Education Statistics.

Whitebook, M., Howes, C., and Phillips, D.A. (1990). *Who cares? Child care teachers and the quality of care in America.* Final report of the National Child Care Staffing Study. Oakland, CA: Child Care Employee Project.

Whitebook, M., Phillips, D., and Howes, C. (1993). *National child care staffing study revisited: Four years in the life of center-based child care.* Oakland, CA: Child Care Employee Project.

recommended resources for further study

Readings

Infant and Toddler Development

Brazelton, T. B. (1992). *Touchpoints: Your child's emotional and behavioral development.* Reading, MA: Addison-Wesley.

Erikson, E. (1950). *Childhood and society.* New York: Norton.

Spock, B. and Rothenberg, M. (1985). *Baby and child care.* New York: E. P. Dutton.

Weiser, M. G. (1991). *Infant/toddler care and education.* Englewood Cliffs, NJ: Prentice-Hall.

White, B. (1975). *The first three years of life.* Englewood Cliffs, NJ: Prentice-Hall.

Group Care for Infants and Toddlers

Bredekamp, S., and Copple, C., (Eds.) (1997). *Developmentally appropriate practice in early childhood programs.* Washington, DC: National Association for the Education of Young Children.

Dittman, L. (Ed.) *The infants we care for.* Washington, DC: National Association for the Education of Young Children.

Godwin, A., and Schrag, L. (1996). *Setting up for infant/toddler care: Guidelines for centers and family child care homes.* Washington, DC: National Association for the Education of Young Children.

Gonzalez-Mena, J. and Eyer, D. W. (1989). *Infants, toddlers and caregivers.* Mt. View, CA: Mayfield.

Lally, R. J., Griffin, A., Fenichel, E., Segal, M., Szanton, El, and Weissbourd, B. (1995). *Caring for infants and toddlers in groups: Developmentally appropriate practice.* Arlington, VA: ZERO TO THREE/National Center.

Raikes, H. (1996). A secure base for babies: Applying attachment concepts to the infant care setting. *Young children,* 51 (5).

Family Child Care

Gonzalez-Mena, J. (1991). *Tips and tidbits: A book for family day care providers.* Washington, DC: National Association for the Education of Young Children.

Kontos, S. (1992). *Family day care: Out of the shadows and into the limelight.* Washington, DC: National Association for the Education of Young Children.

Modigliani, K., Reiff, M., and Jones, S. (1987). *Opening your door to children: How to start a family day care program.* Washington, DC: National Association for the Education of Young Children.

Issues of High Quality Care and Advocacy

Goffin, S. G., and Lombardi, J. (1988). *Speaking out: Early childhood advocacy.* Washington, DC: National Association for the Education of Young Children.

Honig, A. S. (1985). High quality infant/toddler care. *Young children,* 41 (1).

National Association for the Education of Young Children. (1988). *Early childhood program accreditation: A commitment to excellence.* Washington, DC: NAEYC.

Infants and Toddlers with Special Needs

Ross, H. W. (1992). Integrating infants with disabilities? Can "ordinary" caregivers do it? *Young children,* 47 (3).

Segal, M. (1988). *In time and with love: Caring for the special needs baby.* New York: Newmarket Press.

Widerstrom, A. H. (1986). Educating young handicapped children: What can early childhood education contribute? *Childhood education,* 63.

Guidance and Discipline

Greenberg, P. (1991). *Character development: Encouraging self-esteem and self-discipline in infants, toddlers and two-year-olds.* Washington, DC: National Association for the Education of Young Children.

Wittmer, D. S., and Honig, A. S. (1994). Encouraging positive social development in young children. *Young children, 49* (5).

Working with Families of Infants and Toddlers

Gonzalez-Mena, J. (1987). Mrs. Godzilla takes on the child development experts: Perspectives on parent education. *Child care information exchange.*

Jones, E. (Ed.) (1979). *Supporting the growth of infants, toddlers and parents.* Pasadena, CA: Pacific Oaks.

Cultural Sensitivity

Derman-Sparks, L. (1989). *Anti-bias curriculum: Tools for empowering young children.* Washington, DC: National Association for the Education of Young Children.

Gonzalez-Mena, J. (1993). *Multicultural issues in child care.* Mt. View, CA: Mayfield.

Mallory, B. L., and New, R. S. (1994). *Diversity and developmentally appropriate practices: Challenges for early childhood education.* New York: Teachers College Press.

Toilet Learning

American Academy of Pediatrics. (1993). *Toilet training: Guidelines for parents.* Oak Grove Village, IL: Author.

Miller, K. (1997). *Caring for the little ones: Toilet learning.* Child Care Information Exchange.

Videotapes

The Program for Infant/Toddler Caregivers, Video Series, J. Ronald Lally, Executive Producer. California Department of Education, P. O. Box 944271, Sacramento, CA 95812-0271:

1995. *Protective urges: Working with the feelings of parents and caregivers.*

1992. *Essential connections: Ten keys to culturally sensitive child care.*

1991. *Discoveries in infancy: Cognitive development and learning.*

1991. *Together in care: Meeting the intimacy needs of infants and toddlers in groups.*

1989. *Flexible, fearful or feisty: The different temperaments of infants and toddlers.*

1989. *It's not just routine: Diapering, feeding and napping infants and toddlers.*

1989. *The three ages of infancy: Caring for young, mobile and older infants.*

1988. *Space to grow: Creating a child care environment for infants and toddlers.*

1988. *Getting in tune: Creating nurturing relationships with infants and toddlers.*

1987. *Respectfully yours: Magda Gerber's approach to professional infant/toddler care.*

1986. *First move: Welcoming a child to a new caregiving setting.*

National Organizations

Child Development Associate (CDA) Credential Program
The Council for Early Childhood Professional Recognition
1341 G Street, NW, Suite 400
Washington, DC 20005
(202) 265-9090

National Association for the Education of Young Children
1509 16th Street, NW
Washington, DC 20036-1426
(800) 424-2460

National Association of Family Child Care
1331-A Pennsylvania Avenue, NW, Suite 348
Washington, DC 20004
(800) 359-3817

National Black Child Development Institute of America
1023 15th Street, NW, Suite 600
Washington, DC 20005
(202) 387-1281

National Center for the Early Childhood Workforce
733 15th Street, NW
Washington, DC 20005
(202) 737-7700

ZERO TO THREE/The National Center
734 15th Street, NW
Suite 1000
Washington, DC 20005
(800) 899-4301

developmental milestones of children from birth to age 3[1]

	interest in others	self-awareness	motor milestones and eye-hand skills
The Early Months (birth through 8 months)	Newborns prefer the human face and human sound. Within the first 2 weeks, they recognize and prefer the sight, smell, and sound of the principal caregiver.	Sucks fingers of hand fortuitously. Observes own hands. Places hand up as an object comes close to the face as if to protect self.	The young infant uses many complex reflexes; searches for something to suck; holds on when falling; turns head to avoid obstruction of breathing; avoids brightness, strong smells, and pain.
	Social smile and mutual gazing is evidence of early social interaction. The infant can initiate and terminate these interactions.	Looks to the place on body where being touched. Reaches for and grasps toys. Clasps hands together and fingers them.	Puts hand or object in mouth. Begins reaching toward interesting objects.
	Anticipates being lifted or fed and moves body to participate.	Tries to cause things to happen.	Grasps, releases, regrasps, and releases object again.
	Sees adults as objects of interest and novelty. Seeks out adults for play. Stretches arms to be taken.	Begins to distinguish friends from strangers. Shows preference for being held by familiar people.	Lifts head. Holds head up. Sits up without support. Rolls over. Transfers and manipulates objects with hands. Crawls.

[1]Note: This list is not intended to be exhaustive. Many of the behaviors indicated here will happen earlier or later for individual infants. The chart suggests an approximate time when a behavior might appear but it should not be rigidly interpreted.

Often, but not always, the behaviors appear in the order in which they emerge. Particularly for younger infants the behaviors listed in one domain overlap considerably with several other developmental domains. Some behaviors are placed under more than one category to emphasize this interrelationship.

language development/ communication	physical, spatial, and temporal awareness	purposeful action and use of tools	expression of feelings
Cries to signal pain or distress.	Comforts self by sucking thumb or finding pacifier.	Observes own hands.	Expresses discomfort and comfort pleasure unambiguously.
Smiles or vocalizes to initiate social contact.	Follows a slowly moving object with eyes.	Grasps rattle when hand and rattle are both in view.	Responds with more animation and pleasure to primary caregiver than to others.
Responds to human voices. Gazes at faces.	Reaches and grasps toys.	Hits or kicks an object to make a pleasing sight or sound continue.	Can usually be comforted by familiar adult when distressed.
Uses vocal and nonvocal communication to express interest and exert influence.	Looks for dropped toy.	Tries to resume a knee ride by bouncing to get adult started again.	Smiles and activates the obvious pleasure in response to social stimulation. Very interested in people. Shows displeasure at loss of social contact.
Babbles using all types of sounds. Engages in private conversations when alone.	Identifies objects from various viewpoints. Finds a toy hidden under a blanket when placed there while watching.		Laughs aloud (belly laugh).
Combines babbles. Understands names of familiar people and objects. Laughs. Listens to conversations.			Show displeasure or disappointment at loss of toy.
			Expresses several clearly differentiated emotions: pleasure, anger, anxiety or fear, sadness, joy, excitement, disappointment, exuberance.
			Reacts to strangers with soberness or anxiety.

Reprinted with permission, Lally, J. R., Provence, S., Szanton, E., & Weissbourd, B. (1986). Developmentally appropriate care for children from birth to age 3. In S. Bredekamp (Ed.), *Developmentally appropriate practice.* Washington, DC: National Association for the Education of Young Children.

	interest in others	self-awareness	motor milestones and eye-hand skills
crawlers and walkers (8 to 18 months)	Exhibits anxious behavior around unfamiliar adults. Enjoys exploring objects with another as the basis for establishing relationships. Gets others to do things for child's pleasure (wind up toys, read books, get dolls). Shows considerable interest in peers. Demonstrates intense attention to adult language.	Knows own name. Smiles or plays with self in mirror. Uses large and small muscles to explore confidently when a sense of security is offered by presence of caregiver. Frequently checks for caregiver's presence. Has heightened awareness of opportunities to make things happen, yet limited awareness of responsibility for own actions. Indicates strong sense of self through assertiveness. Directs actions of others (e.g., "Sit there!"). Identifies one or more body parts. Begins to use *me, you, I.*	Sits well in chairs. Pulls self up, stands holding furniture. Walks when led. Walks alone. Throws objects. Climbs Stairs. Uses marker on paper. Stoops, trots, can walk backward a few steps.
toddlers and 2 year olds (18 months to 3 years)	Shows increased awareness of being seen and evaluated by others. Sees others as a barrier to immediate gratification. Begins to realize others have rights and privileges. Gains greater enjoyment from peer play and joint exploration. Begins to see benefits of cooperation. Identifies self with children of same age or sex. Is more aware of the feelings of others. Exhibits more impulse control and self-regulation in relation to others. Enjoys small-group activities.	Shows strong sense of self as an individual, as evidenced by "NO" to adult requests. Experiences self as a powerful, potent, creative doer. Explores everything. Becomes capable of self-evaluation and has beginning notions of self (good, bad, attractive, ugly). Makes attempts at self-regulation. Uses names of self and others. Identifies six or more body parts.	Scribbles with marker or crayon. Walks up and down stairs. Can jump off one step. Kicks a ball. Stands on one foot. Threads beads. Draws a circle. Stands and walks on tiptoes. Walks up stairs one foot on each step. Handles scissors. Imitates a horizontal crayon stroke.

language development/ communication	physical, spatial, and temporal awareness	purposeful action and use of tools	expression of feelings
Understands many more words than can say. Looks toward 20 or more objects when named.	Tries to build with blocks.	When a toy winds down, continues the activity manually.	Actively shows affection for familiar persons: hugs, smiles at, runs toward, leans against, and so forth.
Creates long babbled sentences.	If toy is hidden under one of three cloths while child watches, looks under the right cloth for the toy.	Uses a stick as a tool to obtain a toy.	Show anxiety at separation from primary caregiver.
Shakes head no. Says 2 or 3 clear words.	Persists in a search for a desired toy even when toy is hidden under distracting objects such as pillows.	When a music box winds down, searches for the key to wind it up again.	Shows anger focused on people or objects.
Looks at picture books with interest, points to objects.		Brings a stool to use for reaching for something.	Expresses negative feelings.
Uses vocal signals other than crying to gain assistance.	When chasing a ball that rolled under sofa and out the other side, will make a detour around sofa to get ball.	Pushes away someone or something not wanted.	Shows pride and pleasure in new accomplishments.
Begins to use *me, you, I.*	Pushes foot into shoe, arm into sleeve.	Feeds self finger food (bits of fruit, crackers).	Shows intense feelings for parents.
		Creeps or walks to get something or avoid unpleasantness.	Continues to show pleasure in mastery.
		Pushes foot into shoe, arm into sleeve.	Asserts self, indicating strong sense of self.
		Partially feeds self with fingers or spoon.	
		Handles cup well with minimal spilling.	
		Handles spoon well for self-feeding	
Combines words.	Identifies a familiar object by touch when placed in a bag with two other objects.	When playing with a ring-stacking toy, ignores any forms that have no hole. Stacks only rings or other objects with holes.	Frequently displays aggressive feelings and behaviors.
Listens to stories for a short while.			Exhibits contrasting states and mood shifts (stubborn versus compliant).
Speaking vocabulary may reach 200 words.	Uses "tomorrow," "yesterday."	Classifies, labels, and sorts objects by group (hard versus soft, large versus small).	Shows increased fearfulness (dark, monsters, etc).
Develops fantasy in language. Begins to play pretend games.	Figures out which child is missing by looking at children who are present.	Helps dress and undress self.	Expresses emotions with increasing control.
Defines use of many household items.	Asserts independence: "Me do it."		Aware of own feelings and those of others.
Uses compound sentences.	Puts on simple garments such as cap or slippers.		Shows pride in creation and production.
Uses adjectives and adverbs. Recounts events of the day.			Verbalizes feelings more often. Expresses feelings in symbolic play.
			Shows empathic concern for others.

notes

unit 4
fostering mental health in young children

video program: *dealing with feelings*

fostering mental health in young children

unit overview

Read this section before reading the text assignment.

This unit focuses on children's emotional health. After reviewing Erikson's stages of emotional development, characteristics of the mentally healthy child are identified and qualities of the teacher that appear likely to foster the development of such characteristics in the child are reviewed. The unit then discusses and illustrates practical things the teacher can do that will help children achieve healthy emotional development.

unit objectives

Read these objectives before reading the text assignment.

THIS UNIT:

1. Acquaints you with the prevalence of mental illness in our society.
2. Illustrates how Erikson's stages of development can be linked to practical teaching behaviors that help children work through these stages in ways that foster the development of emotional health.
3. Provides you with basic standards for evaluating the emotional behavior of children.
4. Demonstrates the technique of describing and reflecting feelings.
5. Identifies basic standards for evaluating your own behavior in relation to its effect on the emotional self of the child.

text assignment

Read this assignment.

Chapter 6, "Fostering Mental Health in Young Children," *The Whole Child*, Seventh Edition, Joanne Hendrick.

Refer to the Self-Check Questions for Review.

Chapter 6, pp. 154-155.

focus for learning

Read this section before viewing the video program.

It is suggested that you emphasize emotional health rather than illness in this unit. It seems particularly wise to focus thought on what constitutes healthy behavior and how you can help bring it about.

In particular, you will profit from role playing wherein you practice describing the "child's" feelings to him. This should go beyond merely labeling a child's feelings as "angry" or "happy," although labeling is certainly a step in the right direction. It is more effective to describe to the child what he feels like doing, since this kind of interpretation is grasped most easily by very young children. You will most likely need repeated and extensive practice before you attain adequate skill in this area.

The video program, *Dealing with Feelings*, can be a valuable tool in promoting thought and stimulating ideas for role playing and practical experience. Use the following section of **Video-Related Questions** to help you begin to think about some of the important issues that the video program will address. That way, when similar questions are posed in the video program, you can begin to think about what your responses might be. Being an active viewer of the video program will help you to respond to the following **Video-Related Questions for Reflection and Role Play** in a more meaningful way.

video-related questions for reflection and role play

Read these questions before viewing the video program. After viewing the program, respond to all the questions assigned by your instructor by interacting with another person, aloud to yourself or in your journal. Try to find opportunities to role play or practice the approaches illustrated.

1. How could you, as a teacher, develop a relationship of trust with young children? How would your approach differ when relating to infants, toddlers and older preschool children? What elements of this relationship are essential for all young children, regardless of age? Think about and relate any experiences that you may have had that would illustrate these approaches.

2. What are some examples of self-selection activities, intellectually challenging and self-assertive tasks and games that teachers can offer to children? How do these examples help children develop confidence and independence by making choices and being responsible for the outcome? In what ways could

you, as the teacher, provide direction and guidance during these activities? Think of a self-selection activity that you could offer to a child with impaired vision.

3. How could you, as a teacher, encourage 4 and 5 year olds to investigate their world, make plans and carry them out?

4. Find opportunities to role play useful approaches when moderating disputes between children. Find opportunities to practice helping children identify, describe and acknowledge their negative feelings and then express these feelings to the relevant people. Describe to the "child" in a role-playing situation what the child feels like doing and convey to the child that all emotions are acceptable. Communicate to the child that it is okay to talk about her feelings which helps to prevent the child from acting out how she feels. How would you adapt this process when one of the children has a speech problem?

5. Find many opportunities to role play helping children to use words rather than undesirable behaviors to get what they want. It is beneficial for the "teacher" to first calm the "child," then talk over the difficulty and finally help the child return and resolve the situation. Give the child the opportunity to think of a way to make amends in a situation and help only if the child can't think of something.

6. Try to have many role-playing experiences helping a child separate from her family and form an attachment with an adult at school. Share approaches that have been successful in any practical experience that you may have had. Another role-playing experience could be a meeting with a family to solve a separation problem. It is important for the "teacher" to be showing an interest in the "child's" welfare and be open to the "family's" ideas. Make an effort to demonstrate warmth, empathy, understanding and flexibility.

7. What are some ideas for play that would specifically help children express their emotions and understand their feelings without harming others? How could these types of play experiences help a child involve himself more deeply in play?

8. Role play a meeting with parents concerning a child that might require long-term emotional treatment. It is important for "teachers" and "parents" to demonstrate the development of mutual respect. Perhaps you can use as an example a child from your practical experience who had an emotional problem that could not be solved through short-term emergency treatment in school.

predicaments for your consideration

Respond to the predicaments assigned by your instructor with another person, aloud to yourself or in your journal.

*1. Analyze the following example and suggest what the adult might have said instead that would have described the child's feelings to him.

> During self-select time, I was assigned to the woodworking area with hammers, golf tees and styrofoam. Willie's mother had always stayed with him at school and was about to leave him there for the first time.
>
> *Willie's Mom:* "I'll be right back."
>
> *Me:* "Willie, why don't you come and sit with me?"
>
> *Willie:* "No!" (Beginning to get upset.)
>
> *Willie's Mom:* "I'll see you in a little while, Willie."
>
> As his mother left, I took Willie and held him in my lap as he cried and struggled to go after his mother.
>
> *Me:* "Look, you can help me hammer."
>
> *Willie:* "Mommy!"
>
> *Me:* "You can help me, Willie."
>
> *Willie:* "My Mommy!" He cried louder and struggled more than ever. Then he ran off and hovered near the window, trying to see where his mother had gone.

2. The family of a child in your class has made it clear to you that they disagree with your philosophy of encouraging children to express their feelings. As a result of their upbringing and cultural background, they believe that "children should be seen and not heard." They feel their child is "talking back" whenever he attempts to tell them how he is feeling, particularly when he is upset. How could you explain the importance of helping children recognize and express their feelings while still respecting the family's beliefs and honoring their heritage.

* Predicament by Laura McKee, Institute of Child Development, University of Oklahoma, 1991.

3. Analyze the following exchange between two children. Identify which statements are verbal attacks and decide how you would help these children change the verbal attack statements into self-report statements so both children would understand more clearly how the other child is feeling. Then decide how you would help the children resolve the situation, giving the children involved the opportunity to make amends.

Jonah and Rachel are both playing very intently at the puzzle table. They have been choosing and putting together puzzles happily for about 5 minutes. While Rachel is busily looking for her favorite animal puzzle, she accidentally bumps the puzzle Jonah is working on, causing some of it to fall to the floor. Jonah looks at the pieces on the floor in disbelief, then turns to Rachel and begins to yell.

Jonah: "Look what you did, you dummy!"

Rachel: (yelling back) "I didn't mean to!"

Jonah: "You wrecked my puzzle!"

Rachel: "I did not wreck it!"

Jonah: "You made it fall on purpose!"

Rachel: "I did not! (starts to walk away) I'm not playing with you ever again! You're mean!"

Jonah: "Well, I'm not gonna be your friend anymore!"

assignment for students working or volunteering with children

Complete this assignment and submit the written response to your instructor.

The purpose of this project is to help you become more conscious of opportunities that arise when you can be sensitive to what a child is feeling and put this into words for the child. This kind of opportunity actually comes up many times during a day with all ages of people don't think of it as limited to big, dramatic crisis situations. Make a tape recording of such a situation, if possible. This is fairly easy to do during meals, reading or during other child-adult gathering times. If recording is not possible, you'll just have to do your best to remember and write down the dialogue as soon as possible afterward.

The write-up should include an analysis of two situations one that demonstrates an insensitive response and one that demonstrates a sensitive one. For each one of these situations, begin with the following items:

1. Very briefly, sketch in the scene; that is, explain where the incident took place and tell a little about what is going on. Be sure to include the children's ages and names or initials.

2. Write out the conversation, using direct quotations. (Don't say, for example, "He said that he wanted to go to the bathroom." Instead quote him directly. "Jimmy yelled, 'But I gotta go I gotta go pee. You're gonna make me wet my pants.'")

PART A: Example of insensitive response

3. Do 1 and 2 listed above.

4. Then underline the portion where you feel your responses did not reflect the child's feeling or emotion.

5. Substitute what you would say next time that would clearly let him know you have understood what he is feeling and that describes his feelings back to him.

PART B: Example of sensitive response

3. Do 1 and 2 listed above.

4. Underline the dialogue where you reflected the child's feeling.

5. Were you satisfied with this or is there anything you would want to modify about that response the next time?

observational assignment

Complete this assignment and submit your written response to your instructor.

Observe in a preschool and make note of conversations between teachers and children when the adult was trying to be sensitive to the feelings of the child. In each conversation that you heard, how did the teacher respond to the child and what did she say to help the child put his feelings into words? Try to write down as much of each conversation as you can and describe the situation that led to the exchange. Underline the dialogue where the teacher was responding sensitively to the feelings of the child and describing his feelings to him.

Then choose one of the conversations when the adult's responses did not reflect the child's feeling or emotion. Substitute what you would say instead that would clearly let him know you have understood what he is feeling, and describe back to him what he is feeling. Underline the dialogue where you modified what the teacher said and described the child's feeling to him.

references for further reading

Faber, A., & Mazlish, E. (1980). *How to Talk So Kids Will Listen, & Listen So Kids Will Talk.* New York: Avon Books.

Goleman, D. (1995). *Emotional Intelligence.* New York: Bantam Books.

Hyson, M.C. (1994). *The Emotional Development of Young Children: Building an Emotion-Centered Curriculum.* New York: Teachers College Press.

Koplow, L. (1996). *Unsmiling Faces: How Preschools Can Heal.* New York: Teachers College Press.

Samalin, N., & Jablow, M.M. (1987). *Loving Your Child Is Not Enough.* New York: Viking Press.

unit 5
developing self-esteem in young children

video program: *I'm glad I'm me*

developing self-esteem in young children

unit overview

Read this section before reading the text assignment.

This unit stresses an approach intended to help children internalize feelings of self-esteem by developing competence rather than by remaining permanently dependent on praise and recognition supplied by other people.

unit objectives

Read these objectives before reading the text assignment.

THIS UNIT:

1. Provides a definition of self-esteem and explains the difference between esteem that is generated by means of external (extrinsic) rewards and esteem that results from internal (intrinsic) satisfactions.

2. Identifies common teaching practices likely to reduce feelings of self-worth

3. Suggests positive methods of enhancing self-esteem using both extrinsic and intrinsic approaches.

4. Stresses the value of competence, creativity and mastery as being sound ways of instilling long-term feelings of self-worth.

text assignment

Read this assignment.

Chapter 7, "Developing Self-Esteem in Young Children," *The Whole Child*, Seventh Edition, Joanne Hendrick.

*Refer to **Self-Check Questions for Review**.*

Chapter 7, p. 171.

focus for learning

When considering ways to build self-esteem, think beyond the level of complimenting a child. Try to identify common teaching practices that reduce feelings of self-esteem. Explore ways to help children experience the satisfaction of being competent and creative.

Role playing is invaluable in order to deepen your understanding of how to offer unconditional positive regard, express honest recognition and praise, and how to show respect for each child. Take time to reflect and discuss with another student, family member or friend ways to offer children opportunities to develop competence.

The video program, *I'm Glad I'm Me*, can be a valuable tool in promoting thought and stimulating ideas for role playing and practical experience. Use the following section of **Video-Related Questions** to help you begin to think about some of the important issues that the video program will address. That way, when similar questions are posed in the video program, you can begin to think about what your responses might be. Being an active viewer of the video program will help you to respond to the following **Video-Related Questions for Reflection and Role Play** in a more meaningful way.

video-related questions for reflection and role play

Read these questions before viewing the video program. After viewing the program, respond to the questions assigned by your instructor by interacting with another person, aloud to yourself or in your journal. Try to find opportunities to role play or practice the approaches illustrated.

1. How could you, as a caregiver, contribute to the development of self-esteem in infants? How could you provide encouragement and allow these very young children to develop competencies? Try to expand on the thoughts of the caregivers in the video program.

2. How can you, as a teacher, express unconditional positive regard to children? How can you let children know that they are cared for and valued as unique individuals with their own feelings, ideas and qualities? How can you convey to children that you accept their right to be different from teachers and other children?

3. Find opportunities to role play the expression of honest recognition and praise that is based on something a child has specifically achieved. Watch for empty compliments and instead draw attention to something significant the "child" has done.

4. How can you, as a teacher, show children that you respect them? Find opportunities to role play giving children valid choices and then abiding by their decision once the choice is made. Another beneficial role-playing situation is asking a "child's" opinion about something and listening

carefully to his reply. Practice discussing rules with children, which communicates to them that they are important enough to be entitled to an explanation and intelligent enough to comprehend it.

5. How can you, as a teacher, encourage children to feel competent and in control of their environment while still maintaining standards and expectations for children in your classroom? What are some examples of decisions that children can make in the classroom and what might be the consequences of their decisions?

6. What ideas do you have for new and exciting explorations for children that would help them to experience success in many different ways? How can you encourage children to work productively? Think about what you have observed and heard so far in the video program and suggest possible areas of exploration that could stem from the interests of these children.

7. How can you, as a teacher, provide opportunities for children to be challenged and accomplish a difficult task and, at the same time, avoid frustrating situations that can discourage children? How can you be sure to offer appropriately challenging activities in order to help children develop internalized feelings of competence and self-worth? How can cooperative activities help children to develop self-esteem? You may be able to think of examples from your practical experience that would help to illustrate these principles.

8. What ideas do you have for offering children opportunities to explore and express their creative ideas? How can creative activities help children with special needs to develop competency and gain skills? You may be able to think of examples from your practical experience.

9. How could you, as a teacher, support families and parents in enhancing children's self-esteem? How could you present positive methods of developing self-esteem in their children while respecting the parents' views and past practices?

10. How could you, as a teacher, enhance the self-esteem of the children in your class by valuing the cultural traditions of the children and their families? What specific ideas do you have for welcoming family members and encouraging them to share their cultural heritage with the other children and their families?

predicament for your consideration

Respond to this predicament with another person, aloud to yourself or in your journal.

You are now the teacher of a group of 4 year olds, and among the children is a boy who has an artificial arm and a substitute hand that is made of metal and looks a little like Captain Hook's artificial hand. He is also quite lame and clumsy. Even though the other children in the group are genuinely nice to him, he is very self-conscious and thinks no one likes him. He spends most of his time in the book corner, refusing to try to do much of anything else saying, "I'll do it tomorrow," or "My Mother doesn't want me to do that." Do you think this is a case of low self-esteem? Suggest a number of possible ways you could help this child blossom.

assignment for students working or volunteering with children

Complete this assignment and submit the written response to your instructor.

The purpose of this assignment is to help you become more aware of things you are doing that enhance the self-esteem of the children in your care and also to help you become aware of behaviors you might wish to avoid in the future.

Pair off with another student and do a turn and turn-about observation of each other's behavior during snack time. Make notes during your observation to share together later on.

Incidents to look out for and note include:

1. Talking about a child over her head to a third person (perhaps even to the observer).
2. Utilizing competition and comparison to induce good behavior.
3. Praising or thanking a child.
4. Encouraging a child to develop a skill so she feels more competent.
5. Doing something for a child when she could have done it for herself.
6. Providing situations where the child was encouraged to make a decision for herself.

After you have both made your observations, find time to discuss the behaviors that would enhance the children's self-esteem as well as how you would adapt observed behaviors that are likely to reduce feelings of esteem.

observational assignment

Complete this assignment and submit your written response to your instructor.

The purpose of this assignment is to help students become more aware of things that teachers do to enhance the self-esteem of the children in their class and also to become aware of behaviors teachers might avoid in the future.

Observe in a preschool classroom and observe teacher behaviors. Make notes during your observation. Incidents to look out for and note include:

1. Talking about a child over her head to a third person.
2. Utilizing competition and comparison to induce good behavior.
3. Praising or thanking a child.
4. Encouraging a child to develop a skill so she feels more competent.
5. Doing something for a child when she could have done it for herself.
6. Providing situations where the child was encouraged to make a decision for herself.

After your observation, find time to reflect on the positive behaviors that you observed as well as how you would change the observed behaviors likely to reduce feelings of self-esteem. Make note of your suggestions for improving these approaches.

references for further reading

Andrew, C., & Tracy, N. (1996). First Steps Toward Competence: Promoting Self-Esteem and Confidence in Young Children With Disabilities. In L.E. Powers, G.H.S. Singer, & J. Sowers (Eds.), *On the Road to Autonomy: Promoting Self-Competence in Children and Youth With Disabilities.* Baltimore, MD: Paul H. Brookes.

Hewitt, D., & Heideman, S. (1998). *The Optimistic Classroom: Creative Ways to Give Children Hope.* St. Paul, MN: Redleaf.

Hopkins, S., & Winerts, J. (1990). *Discover the World: Empowering Children to Value Themselves, Others, and the Earth.* Philadelphia, PA: New Society.

Owens, K. (1995). *Raising Your Child's Inner Self-esteem: The Authoritative Guide From Infancy Through the Teen Years.* New York: Plenum Press.

unit 6
communicating with families

video program: *listening to families*

communicating with families

unit overview

Read this section before reading the text assignment.

This unit focuses on getting along with families and genuinely welcoming them into the school. This unit also touches on initial problems that may interfere with communication between parents and teachers and then offers some matter-of-fact suggestions for improving communication and counseling both in informal settings and within more formal conference structures. The most common crises that children experience are discussed, and suggestions on basic things families and teachers can do to help themselves and the children are offered.

unit objectives

Read these objectives before reading the text assignment.

THIS UNIT:

1. Suggests ways of establishing good relationships between teachers and parents.

2. Discusses problems and situations that interfere with good communication with families.

3. Provides practical suggestions about how to carry out effective guidance work.

4. Acquaints you with basic principles of crisis management.

5. Provides information about specific crises likely to affect young children.

6. Provides specific recommendations for dealing with specific crises in as productive a way as possible.

text assignment

Read this assignment.

Chapter 3, "What Parents Need" and Chapter 8, "Tender Topics: Helping Children Master Emotional Crises," *The Whole Child*, Seventh Edition, Joanne Hendrick.

*Refer to the **Self-Check Questions for Review**.*

Chapter 3, p. 73.
Chapter 8, p. 205.

focus for learning

Read this section before viewing the video program.

One of the most successful ways to enrich and deepen counseling skills is a technique suggested by Carl Rogers wherein students pair together and practice their listening and responding skills. While another student discusses any problem she cares to, your task is to listen and respond in your own words, describing back to her what she is feeling and has said. It is only after this response that you may make any additional response or suggestion you wish to. After 10 minutes or so, stop and talk over how well you are doing and then shift roles so that you have a chance to outline your problem.

A second useful focus is to talk and think about how you really feel about talking to parents. Many teachers are apprehensive about doing this, and sharing this anxiety can help reduce its potency.

Enrich your knowledge and understanding of specific crises that young children may encounter in any way that you can and become aware of sources of help for specific crises within the community. Talking over actual situations you may have encountered in your work with families is also helpful. It is, of course, necessary to maintain careful confidentiality in such discussions.

The video program, *Listening to Families*, can be a valuable tool in promoting thought and stimulating ideas for role-playing and practical experience. Use the following section of **Video-Related Questions** to help you begin to think about some of the important issues that the video program will address. That way, when similar questions are posed in the video, you can begin to think about what your responses might be. Being an active viewer of the video program will help you to respond to the following **Video-Related Questions for Reflection and Role Play** in a more meaningful way.

video-related questions for reflection and role play

Read these questions before viewing the video program. After viewing the program, respond to all these questions by interacting with another person, aloud to yourself or in your journal. Try to find opportunities to role play or practice the approaches illustrated.

1. Work on developing your "active listening" skills by role-playing informal discussions between "parents" and "teachers." Be sure you and your fellow student or friend are using body language that communicates they are

listing and interested. Think of different concerns that parents may have and explore these in "parent-teacher" discussions.

2. Respond to the scene in the video program where the teacher is not "actively listening" to the parent by suggesting how the teacher might react in a more appropriate or productive way to the parent. How could the four "active listening" skills be used in this situation?

3. Brainstorm possible solutions to the situations presented in the video program or reflect on solutions to situations that you may have encountered in your work with parents of young children. If you have had limited experience with families of young children, think of possible problems with families that preschool teachers may encounter and brainstorm possible solutions to these.

4. What kinds of issues or situations have you found to be most upsetting to you in your experience with parents of young children? Think about or discuss with another student or friend your "flashpoints," how you have responded to these situations in the past and how you might better respond in the future.

5. Try to find opportunities to role play interacting with a child about a family crisis. Set up role-playing situations with another student, friend or family member. Try to explore children's feelings and teachers' reactions to various crises: new baby, divorce, hospitalization, death. Practice listening to the "child," helping her express her feelings and worries about what is happening and being truthful about the situation.

6. What ideas do you have for imaginative play and relaxation activities that can help children express their feelings and relieve the stress caused by a family crisis. Think of creative activities for various crisis situations that you could offer to a child in these situations.

7. How would a teacher have to respond differently to a child with Down Syndrome who has a new baby brother and is upset at the change in his life at home? How could a teacher help a child with speech difficulties who is upset about her mother's long-term hospitalization and is having trouble talking about her feelings? What choices could these children be given in a classroom situation to help them feel more in control of their lives? What role could school routines play in helping these children?

8. How can teachers best communicate respect to the parents of the children in their class? Reflect on or discuss ways that you, as a preschool teacher, could let parents know that their opinions, feelings and privacy are important to you? Why is this especially important during a crisis situation?

9. Why is communicating respect so important when the family is from a culture different from the teacher's? In what ways can you, as a teacher, best communicate respect to parents from different ethnic or cultural backgrounds?

predicaments for your consideration

Respond to these predicaments with another person, aloud to yourself or in your journal.

1. You are an infant caregiver in a child care center and you are concerned that a 6 month-old infant in your care is undernourished and often in need of a bath. He is too thin, always hungry and has developed severe diaper rash that is not being treated at home. How can you approach the parents of this child and help them take better care of their child without offending them?

2. You are now head teacher in a class of 3 year olds. One afternoon a mother is a half hour late picking her child up. When you ask why she is late she snarls, "None of your business" and yanks her child out the door. How would you handle this situation?

3. A child comes to school acting listless and looking pale and washed out. At nap time, when he undresses, you find he has several bruises on his chest and around his arms, and he complains that his neck hurts. There has been a previous occasion where he arrived with a bump on his head and a black eye, which his mother said were due to his falling down a flight of steps. Under these circumstances, do you think it wisest to approach the parent with your concern, or are there alternative solutions that should be explored? If the parent, in your judgment, should not be approached, what agencies in your own community would be the most appropriate and effective ones to contact?

assignment for students working or volunteering with children

Complete this assignment and submit the written response to your instructor.

Make arrangements to observe a teacher-parent conference and make as many mental notes as possible during that time. It is wise to go immediately to some quiet place and write these notes out as soon as you can to keep memories fresh in your mind.

The purpose of this observation is not so much to attend to what was said, the verbal content of the conference, but to look at the structure of the conference and the feelings and behavior of the participants. Look beyond the content to the dynamics of the interaction.

It will be necessary to obtain the permission of the teacher and the parents involved. Most teachers will be able to help arrange this observation with parents with whom they have a good relationship and who know they can arrange a more private talk with the teacher at another time, if necessary.

Please note with special care the following aspects and document your answers with actual examples:

1. Who began the encounter, and what did that person do to open it?

2. How did changes of subject take place?

3. In your opinion, how much real listening did each participant do? How could you tell?

4. Could you perceive any examples of reflecting and describing feelings by either person?

5. Did any real problem solving appear to take place?

observational assignment

Complete this assignment and submit the written response to your instructor.

Make arrangements to observe in several classrooms at a child care center and note the different ways that teachers are communicating with parents. Be sure to observe any informal conversations about the children at arrival and departure times. Were information and observations shared with parents about children and their experiences during the day? Are notes, newsletters or any other form of written communication used regularly by the teachers? What kind of information is shared with parents this way? Do the teachers use phone calls to communicate with the parents and for what reason? Are teachers communicating with parents through the children's work and/or words displayed in the classroom?

During and after your observations and conversations with the teachers at the child care center, summarize your findings and then suggest other ways that teachers could communicate with parents at that center.

references for further reading

Diffily, D., & Morrison, K. (Eds.). (1996). *Family Friendly Communication for Early Childhood Programs.* Washington, DC: National Association for the Education of Young Children.

Hildebrand, V., Phenice, L.A., Gray, M.M., & Hines, R.P. (2000). *Knowing and Serving Diverse Families.* Upper Saddle River, NJ: Merrill/Prentice Hall.

Miller, K. (1996). *The Crisis Manual for Early Childhood Teachers: How to Handle the Really Difficult Problems.* Beltsville, MD: Gryphon House.

Oehlberg, B. (1996). *Making It Better: Activities for Children Living in a Stressful World.* St. Paul, MN: Redleaf.

notes

the whole child **student guide**

unit 7
working with
exceptional children

video program: *everybody's special*

working with exceptional children
unit overview

Read this section before reading the text assignment.

The implications of the Individuals with Disabilities Education Act (IDEA) and the Americans with Disabilities Act (ADA) for people working at the preschool level are explored in Unit 7. This unit also discusses humane, effective ways of approaching parents when a referral for special help seems to be necessary and also includes advice on how the teacher should function as a member of the transdisciplinary team.

Advice on getting started with a child who has a disability is provided as well as general recommendations for working with such youngsters. This unit also focuses on specific disabilities such as vision difficulties, attention deficit disorder, convulsive seizures, sickle-cell anemia, emotional disturbance, autism, intellectual delay and giftedness.

unit objectives

Read these objectives before reading the text assignment.

THIS UNIT:

1. Helps you feel more comfortable about having children with disabilities in your classroom.

2. Provides you with a basic understanding of how to bring about referrals when these are necessary.

3. Makes it clear that it is important for teachers to work as team members when serving children with disabilities.

4. Provides you with fundamental principles that are effective to use when working with children who have a variety of disabilities.

5. Provides you with entry-level information about specific disabilities as well as a resource list for obtaining more detailed information.

6. Explains the implications of federal law as it relates to the education of preschool children with disabilities.

text assignment

Read this assignment.

Chapter 9, "Welcoming Children Who May Have Special Educational Requirements into the Life of the School," *The Whole Child*, Seventh Edition, Joanne Hendrick.

Refer to the Self-Check Questions for Review.

Chapter 9, pp. 241-242.

focus for learning

Read this section before viewing the video program.

Since the passage of IDEA and ADA, it has become essential that teachers of young children are comfortable with and able to help all children including those with special needs. It is important for you to honestly reflect on your feelings about children with disabilities in order to come to terms with them. Consistent contact with exceptional preschoolers is the most effective way for you to understand that such children can generally be successfully included in children's centers.

The video program, *Everybody's Special*, can be a valuable tool in promoting thought and stimulating ideas for role-playing and practical experience. Use the following section of **Video-Related Questions** to help you begin to think about some of the important issues that the video program will address. That way, when similar questions are posed in the video, you can begin to think about what your responses might be. Being an active viewer of the video program will help you to respond to the following **Video-Related Questions for Reflection and Role Play** in a more meaningful way.

video-related questions for reflection and role play

Read these questions before viewing the video program. After viewing the program, respond to all these questions by interacting with another person, aloud to yourself or in your journal. Try to find opportunities to role play or practice the approaches illustrated.

1. Try to find opportunities to role play a discussion with a family of a child who may have a physical, emotional or developmental condition that requires intervention. You can use the children in the video program as

examples or children whom you have known or observed in your own experience. Be sure to give specific reasons and examples why the child may need special help. It's important that you learn to gently and clearly explain the reasons for your concern in order to minimize defensive reactions of family members. Make sure that you are describing behavior and not trying to diagnose the cause.

2. What are some important referral resources for children with special needs in the community where you live? Be sure that you know how to identify and contact appropriate state agencies, local school districts, public health nurses and family physicians once family members agree that special help is needed.

3. What are some ways that an infant might demonstrate that he has a condition that requires special attention? Try to brainstorm possible behaviors or signs to watch out for when caring for infants.

4. Try to find the opportunity to discuss or reflect on the Individuals with Disabilities Education Act and the Americans with Disabilities Act. Make sure that you thoroughly understand these laws and their implications for preschool children and teachers.

5. What are your feelings and/or experiences with programs that integrate children with special needs into typical early childhood settings and programs that are specifically for children with special needs? What benefits and limitations are there for either type of program?

6. Find an opportunity to role play interactions with children who are moderately delayed learners. Be sure you are using concrete examples, definite rules and plenty of positive reinforcement. The "teacher" should be encouraging the "child" to use speech whenever possible and show the child what he means by demonstrating it.

7. Think about ways that teachers can focus on the strengths of children with special needs and not their disabilities. You can refer to children from your own experiences and think how you might help these children to recognize their own abilities.

predicaments for your consideration

Respond to these predicaments with another person, aloud to yourself or in your journal.

1. The teacher of a 4 year-old class next door to your room is about to welcome a child who wears a hearing aid and uses sign language to communicate. During a staff meeting, she brushes aside the concerns expressed about possible problems this might produce by telling everyone that, "After all, this

kid is just like everyone else. I bet the children don't notice any difference. We'll treat him just the same way."

What are the pros and cons of this approach? What advice would you give this teacher about effective ways to integrate that youngster into the class?

2. Shanna is a 3 year-old child in your group who has a mild physical disability that requires a physical therapist to work with her once a week during self-select time. The physical therapist suggests that every time you see Shanna sitting in group using incorrect body positioning, you should put a red dot on the little report card you send home with her each day. When she positions herself correctly, you should put a gold star on the report card. You've gone along with this recommendation but you do not feel comfortable with this kind of teaching. To make matters worse, this past week many of the other children have wanted to know why they can't have gold stars, too!

What would you do to resolve this situation?

assignment for students working or volunteering with children

Complete this assignment and submit the written response to your instructor.

Make arrangements to spend one half-day with a child who has a disability in your school. Use various developmental checklists and observations to help you identify some areas in which the child needs help and can profit from instruction. Discuss these possibilities with the teacher in the classroom and settle on two objectives to work on.

Prepare a lesson plan for the child. The lesson plan should include the two learning objectives, activities planned and the purpose of each activity.

observational assignment

Complete this assignment and submit the written response to your instructor.

Make arrangements to observe preschool children with disabilities, either in children's centers with children who are not disabled or in programs only for children with special needs. Make note of how the disabled children are interacting socially with other children with special needs or with those who are not disabled. Children with any type or degree of disability can be included. Also make note of the activities that the children with special needs were able to participate in and also those they were not able to enjoy because of their disability.

For each child observed, write up a brief report with the child's name and age, type of program, other children in the class and summary of your observations. For each child, answer the following questions:

1. What could you do to help this child interact with the other children in the class? How could you help the other children understand this child's disability and include her in their play?

2. What changes in the activities and environment would you make to help this child to participate more freely?

3. What new activities would you introduce to this child to help her acquire the skills she needs or pursue an interest?

references for further reading

Bricker, D., & Cripe, J.J.W. (1992). *An Activity-Based Approach to Early Intervention.* Baltimore, MD: Paul H. Brookes.

Cook, R.E., Tessier, A., & Klein, M.D. (2000). *Adapting Early Childhood Curricula for Children in Inclusive Settings* (5th ed.). Upper Saddle River, NJ: Merrill/Prentice Hall.

Rab, V.Y., Wood, K.I., & Taylor, J.M. (1995). *Child Care and the ADA.* Baltimore, MD: Paul H. Brookes.

Phelps, L.A. (Ed.). (1998). *Health-Related Disorders in Children and Adolescents.* Washington, DC: American Psychological Association.

unit 8
developing social competence
in young children

video program: *getting along together*

developing social competence in young children

unit overview

Read this section before reading the text assignment.

There are a multitude of social learning skills that children need to acquire in the early years, and the material in this unit selects seven of the most vital ones for in-depth discussion. Each of these skills is cast in terms of a goal and is accompanied by some down-to-earth suggestions about how you can help young children move toward that goal.

unit objectives

Read these objectives before reading the text assignment.

THIS UNIT:

1. Provides a brief outline of the social development of young children and what these findings imply for teaching.

2. Identifies seven age-appropriate social goals to work toward with young children.

3. Suggests effective methods of helping children learn the social skills related to each of the seven goals.

text assignment

Read this assignment.

Chapter 10, "Developing Social Competence in Young Children," *The Whole Child*, Seventh Edition, Joanne Hendrick.

*Refer to the **Self-Check Questions for Review**.*

Chapter 10, p. 268.

focus for learning

Read this section before viewing the video program.

The subject of social competence often has powerful emotional overtones. For example, the concept of how to teach generosity is often interpreted as teaching children how to share. Try to get together with other students in order to think about and discuss your own philosophies on teaching positive social behavior and how these can be implemented in your teaching.

The video program, *Getting Along Together*, can be a valuable tool in promoting thought and stimulating ideas for role playing and practical experience. Use the following section of **Video-Related Questions** to help you begin to think about some of the important issues that the video program addresses. That way, when similar questions are posed in the video program, you can begin to think about what your responses might be. Being an active viewer of the video program will help you to respond to the following **Video-Related Questions for Reflection and Role Playing** in a more meaningful way.

video-related questions for reflection and role playing

Read these questions before viewing the video program. After viewing the program, respond to the questions assigned by your instructor by interacting with another person, aloud to yourself or in your journal. Try to find opportunities to role play or practice the approaches illustrated.

1. How could you, as an infant caregiver, lay the foundation for trust by ensuring that each infant's needs are being met? How does consistent care by the same caregivers help infants to form secure attachments? What sorts of things could you, as an infant caregiver, do to help the child become actively involved in the exploration of her immediate environment and the other people in her world?

2. How could you, as a teacher, maintain open communication with parents of infants and help parents appreciate and respond to their child's unique qualities? Try to find opportunities to role play these interactions with parents when you are sharing your experiences with the baby and discussing his development.

3. What are some different ways that you, as a teacher, could model positive social behavior for children? The video program mentions being considerate

and using calm words instead of yelling. What other ideas do you have or what examples from your practical experiences have been effective?

4. How could you, as a teacher, help children receive satisfaction from acting in socially desirable ways? Try to find opportunities to role play giving attention and praise to children in ways that enhance their sense of satisfaction from within. Learn to phrase your comments so that the "child" understands that it feels good to help other people.

5. Try to find the opportunity to discuss with other students the benefits of "sharing from the heart" as discussed in the text and video program and your experiences with "turn-taking." What situations involving teacher regulated "sharing" can you relate from your practical experiences? If you have observed situations when children were allowed to use toys and equipment until they felt ready to pass them on to another, what were the results?

6. How could you, as a teacher, encourage children to develop empathy, to understand how another person feels? Find opportunities to practice linking a child's experience to the prior experience of another, e.g., "Remember when ___ happened to you? That may be how ___ feels." Understand that this approach is more desirable than "How would you feel if..." What ideas do you have for pretend play and role-playing activities for children that may help them to develop empathy and understand how other people feel?

7. What specific ways could you, as a teacher, help children include children with special needs in their play? If you have had experiences helping children with disabilities fit into the life of the classroom, what approaches have been successful?

8. How could you, as a teacher, give children opportunities to learn to cooperate with each other to accomplish something together? Brainstorm ways that cooperative games and activities can be included in the preschool curriculum.

predicaments for your consideration

Respond to the predicaments assigned by your instructor with another person, aloud to yourself or in your journal.

1. You are now a teacher who is in charge of a group of 4 year olds and this group includes a youngster named Susan who has been diagnosed as being "partially sighted." In her case this means that when she wears her glasses, she sees large objects, particularly when there is good contrast between dark and light ones. She needs to hold things very close to her face if the object is

small, and she has normal intelligence. She loves going down the slide but is afraid of using the swings. She never plays in the sand box because she fears other children will throw sand in her eyes. Despite the fact she sees better with her glasses on, she often takes them off and leaves them wherever she was last playing. She says the glasses make her nose hurt, look funny and she hates them.

List the 5 "P's" mentioned in the book as being particularly important to apply when teaching social skills to children who have disabilities. Explain how, as the teacher, you would apply each of these principles when working with Susan.

2. The family of a new 4-year-old boy in your class has made it clear that it disagrees with your views on what is socially desirable behavior for boys of that age. They have taught their child to always hit back when he is hit by another child. They have also told their son that "boys don't cry," so he feels humiliated when he does cry in school and makes fun of other boys when they cry. How would you explain to this family the rationale for your approach to encouraging the development of socially healthy behaviors while still honoring their very different cultural values?

assignment for students working or volunteering with children

Complete this assignment and submit the written response to your instructor.

The purpose of this assignment is to help you improve your ability to generate positive social interaction between children. Make an audio or video tape recording of a group of children while they are involved in a social situation with you. This interaction has to be taped to be helpful for you later. Next, you should review the tape and select the most interesting parts of the dialogue to write down, complete with the actions that accompanied the dialogue. Finally, you should analyze it according to the written assignment described below.

Either use the recorder yourself or ask a friend to do the recording for you. Remember that the friend should fade into the background as much as possible. Incidentally, if you are disappointed with your first recording, do as many as you like. You may use the best examples or you may include a particularly bad one if you prefer a change of pace!

Some examples of positive social goals include:

1. Encouraging one child to help another person in some way.

2. Encouraging a child to use alternative ways of getting what she wants (in place of some "negative" way of reaching her goal.)

3. Helping a child gain insight into how another person feels.

4. Helping children work cooperatively to accomplish something together.

5. Helping children solve a situation involving sharing.

WRITTEN ASSIGNMENT

1. Play through the recording and select portions that fit any of the goals listed above.

2. Choose two episodes to discuss. Handle the write-up of each episode separately.

3. Describe each situation briefly and record all the dialogue.

4. At the end of each episode, answer the following questions:

    a. What social goal were you hoping to accomplish?

    b. How old were the children in the situations? Looking back, do you think your goal was realistic for them considering their age?

    c. What did you do or say that contributed to a positive result?

    d. What did you do or say that didn't work out as well as you had hoped?

    e. If the children did react positively, then what did you do to reinforce the desirable behavior? How did you make it more likely the child will want to behave in a socially desirable way again?

    f. If you had a skilled mentor looking over your shoulder in this situation, what advice do you think the mentor would give you about handling it next time?

observational assignment

Complete this assignment and submit your written response to your instructor.

Go to a playground and observe preschool children playing together. Look for situations when children are interacting and could use the help of an adult to make the interaction a more positive social experience for all the children involved. Make note of a situation where you, as the adult, could help these children achieve at least one of the following positive social goals:

1. Encouraging one child to help another person in some way.

2. Encouraging a child to use alternative ways of getting what she wants (in place of some "negative" way of reaching her goal.)

3. Helping a child gain insight into how another person feels.

4. Helping children work cooperatively to accomplish something together.

5. Helping children solve a situation involving sharing.

WRITTEN ASSIGNMENT

1. Describe the situation that you witnessed, being careful to note as much of the dialogue as you possibly can.

2. What social goal would you hope to help the children accomplish in this situation?

3. How old do you think the children are? Is your goal realistic for them, considering their age?

4. What would you do or say that would contribute to a positive result? Be specific.

5. If the children do react positively, what would you do to reinforce the desirable behavior? How would you make it more likely the child will want to behave in a socially desirable way again? Be specific.

references for further reading

Read, K.H. (1996). Initial Support Through Guides to Speech and Action. In K.M. Paciorek & J.H. Munro (Eds.), *Sources: Notable Selections in Early Childhood Education*. Guilford, CT: Dushkin.

Witmer, D.S., & Honig, A.S. (1996). Encouraging Positive Social Development in Young Children. In K.M. Paciorek & J.H. Munro (Eds.), *Early Childhood Education 96/97*. Guilford, CT: Dushkin.

Wolf, C.P. (Ed.). (1986). *Connecting: Friendship in the Lives of Young Children and Their Teachers*. Redmond, WA: Exchange Press.

notes

unit 9
helping young children
establish self-dicipline
and self-control

video program: *building inner controls*

helping young children establish self-discipline and self-control

unit overview

Read this section before reading the text assignment.

The topic of discipline is one that worries students the most because they are afraid of losing control and not knowing what to do next. This unit equips you with ideas and techniques that will help you control the children, and at the same time enable the children to gradually achieve control over themselves by fostering the development of inner controls. Aggression is also discussed as well as forms of control that teachers should avoid when dealing with aggressive behavior. Activities that can be included in the curriculum to permit children to express aggressive feelings in acceptable ways will be illustrated.

unit objectives

Read these objectives before reading the text assignment.

THIS UNIT:

1. Informs students about how moral development takes place and tells them what they can do to facilitate that process in young children.

2. Provides basic guidelines on how to control children in a reasonable way.

3. Prepares students for what to do when a discipline crisis occurs.

4. Outlines the six basic steps for handling children who continue to misbehave.

5. Identifies undesirable methods of dealing with aggression.

6. Explains that not all aggression should be discouraged.

text assignment

Read this assignment.

Chapter 11, "Helping Young Children Establish Self-Discipline and Self-Control" and Chapter 12, "Aggression: What To Do About It," *The Whole Child*, Seventh Edition, Joanne Hendrick.

Refer to Self-Check Questions for Review.

Chapter 11, p. 292.
Chapter 12, pp. 311-312.

focus for learning

Read this section before viewing the video program.

It is helpful to begin this topic by thinking over reasons why children misbehave and what to do about it. Think about specific instances you have witnessed in a preschool or in public that have troubled you. This is a good time to come to terms with your own feelings about aggression and identify how you cope with such impulses in yourself, because you will tend to teach children to cope with this feeling in the same manner as you do. It will be helpful to become aware of alternative actions you can propose to children that enable them to obtain what they want without resorting to hurting other people.

The video program, *Building Inner Controls*, can be a valuable tool in promoting thought and stimulating ideas for role playing and practical experience. Use the following section of **Video-Related Questions** to help you begin to think about some of the important issues that the video program will address. That way, when similar questions are posed in the video, you can begin to think about what your responses might be. Being an active viewer of the video program will help you to respond to the following **Video-Related Questions for Reflection and Role Play** in a more meaningful way.

video-related questions for reflection and role play

Read these questions before viewing the video program. After viewing the program, respond to all these questions by interacting with another person, aloud to yourself or in your journal. Try to find opportunities to role play or practice the approaches illustrated.

1. How could you, as a teacher, give children opportunities for decision-making? Brainstorm different situations in which children can make decisions in the preschool environment.

2. Brainstorm examples of situations that could occur at a child care center when children are experiencing the consequences of their decisions.

3. Practice giving the reason behind various rules that would be enforced at most child care centers. What should the non-negotiable rules be?

4. How would you react differently in a discipline situation with an 18 month old and with a 5 year old? How do their motivations differ and to what approach do they respond the best? Think of examples, possibly from your experience, and role play these approaches, if possible.

5. Brainstorm examples of practical ways to stop discipline situations before they start, such as: rewarding positive behavior; warning ahead; not giving up in a discipline situation; and emphasizing the positive by telling the child the correct thing to do. Role play with a friend, family member or student study partner, if possible.

6. Practice helping children put their feelings into words by role playing with another adult. Phrase your descriptions tentatively until the "teacher" is sure about the "child's" motives. Then evaluate how well feelings were described.

7. Find opportunities to practice the six steps for immediate self-control. Be sure the "teacher" is making it clear to the "child" that her behavior is up to her. Role play this process from beginning to end, whenever possible.

8. What are your feelings and experiences with the "time-out" chair?

9. Think about your own flashpoints and, perhaps, the reasons for them. Practical experiences can be used for a reference. What behaviors anger or bother you the most?

10. Think of examples of a situation where children could be encouraged to negotiate a solution to a problem. You could role play with two other people in different situations or practice in your personal experience, if possible.

11. Think about certain behaviors that you see among children and decide what the pay-off is for the child. The behavior can be that which would be considered hostile or aggressive, or not.

predicaments for your consideration

Respond to these predicaments with another person, aloud to yourself or in your journal.

1. Margie is riding the tricycle and invites Jeanette to put her doll in the back of the trike wagon, but Jeanette refuses. This refusal makes Margie angry and she bumps Jeanette and the doll with the trike. Jeanette drops the doll and Margie drives over it, crushing one of its arms. Jeanette begins to cry. The teacher says, "Oh, Margie! That's awful! How would you feel if you were Jeanette's doll, and she ran over you with a trike?"

   How would you approach this situation and what would you suggest saying to simplify the teacher's response and, possibly, build a feeling of empathy for Jeanette in Margie's heart?

2. A new child has joined your class whose family has just moved from another country. The family has made it clear to you that they believe in using physical punishment when their child misbehaves and suggests that you do

the same. As a teacher in this situation, how could you respond to this family? How can you manage to welcome this family to the school and respect their culture and philosophies while practicing your own approach to teaching children about self-control and self-discipline?

3. Lily and Emily are playing in the housekeeping corner and a squabble develops over what they will feed their doll family for breakfast. Lily wants to serve fruit and cinnamon toast, but Emily is holding out for her favorite oatmeal with raisins. In order to prevent Lily from making toast, Emily grabs the plastic bread and runs to the block corner with it, waving it over her head as she runs. Meanwhile, Lily grabs the cereal pan and yells she's going to dump it out if Emily doesn't bring the bread right back so she can make cinnamon toast.

Your goal, as their teacher, is to teach the girls alternative ways of getting what they want. What alternatives are the girls using already? What additional alternatives might you suggest?

assignments for students working or volunteering with children

Complete the assignment(s) required by your instructor and submit the written response to him/her.

1. Keep a private journal for a week, noting any situations in which you had to see to it that a child did what she was supposed to do, even though she didn't want to. Be as honest with yourself as you can be.

   Write down how you felt about each situation. Did you feel anxious? Nervous? Angry? Determined? Grim? Irritated? Were you able to bring the matter to a successful conclusion? How did the youngster appear to feel about you afterward? If you felt unable to deal with the problem, what happened then? Did you ask for help? Allow the child to run off? Give in and let the child do as he or she wished?

   At the end of the semester, keep a second week's record paying attention to the same things you did before. Note how your attitudes and approaches changed over that period of time.

2. Two 4 year-old girls are struggling over who should be allowed to use the parasol. As they yank it back and forth, they are tearfully shouting at each other, and things are rapidly threatening to get worse and more violent.

Using this as an example, describe how (1) an authoritarian teacher, (2) an inconsistent teacher and (3) an overly permissive teacher might handle this situation. Write this part of the assignment up before proceeding to the second part.

Now be on the lookout for the next time you have to handle an aggressive situation, describe what happened, and analyze how you dealt with it. Identify which one of the above behavior patterns (if any) your response coincides with most closely.

observational assignments

Complete the assignment(s) chosen by your instructor and submit your written response to him/her.

1. Observe in a preschool and note ways that the room is set up and teachers respond to the children that could serve to minimize discipline situations and reduce frustration among the children. Write about three ways that the center can improve their classroom set-up. Also, suggest three ways that the teachers can respond better to the children in order to avoid discipline situations and reduce frustration.

2. Go to a park, mall or grocery store and observe parents with young children. Note any situations in which a parent tried to get a child to do something he or she was supposed to do, even though the child didn't want to.

   How did the parent appear to feel about each situation? Did they seem to feel anxious? Nervous? Angry? Determined? Grim? Irritated? Were they able to bring the matter to a successful conclusion? How did the youngster appear to feel about them afterward? If the parent was unable to deal with the problem, what happened then? Did the parent allow the child to run off? Did they give in and let the child do as he or she wished?

3. Go to a playground and observe young children playing. Note any situations where children are wanting to use the same piece of playground equipment at the same time or maybe the same toy in the sand box. If any situation escalates to a fight over who gets to play on a certain swing or rocking animal, describe how (1) an authoritarian teacher, (2) an inconsistent teacher and (3) an overly permissive teacher might handle this situation.

   How would you have handled an aggressive situation such as this? Identify which one of the above behavior patterns (if any) your response coincides with most closely? How did the adult with the children in that particular situation respond?

references for further reading

Carlsson-Paige, N. & Levin, D.E. (1998). *Before Push Comes to Shove: Building Conflict Resolution Skills With Children.* St. Paul, MN: Redleaf.

Hewitt, F. (1995). *So This Is Normal Too?* St. Paul, MN: Redleaf.

Kaiser, B., & Rasminsky, J.S. (1999). *Meeting the Challenge: Effective Strategies for Challenging Behaviors in Early Childhood Environments.* Ottawa, Ontario: Canadian Child Care Federation.

Saifer, S. (1990). *Practical Solutions to Practically Every Problem: The Early Childhood Teacher's Manual.* St. Paul, MN: Toys 'n Things Press.

notes

the whole child **student guide**

unit 10
providing cross-cultural, nonsexist education

video program: *respecting diversity*

providing cross-cultural, nonsexist education

unit overview

Read this section before reading the text assignment.

This unit considers two approaches that should be included when one is considering the questions of multicultural and nonsexist curriculum: (1) recognizing and honoring cultural/ethnic differences and differences related to gender and (2) emphasizing the needs and similarities that all human beings, regardless of race or gender, have in common.

unit objectives

Read these objectives before reading the text assignment.

THIS UNIT:

1. Provides evidence that even young children are aware of racial and gender differences.
2. Defines and explains two approaches that are helpful in teaching about cultural and gender differences and similarities.
3. Provides you with many ideas and suggestions about ways to incorporate multiethnic, nonsexist teaching in the classroom.

text assignment

Read this assignment.

Chapter 13, "Providing Cross-Cultural, Nonsexist Education," *The Whole Child,* Seventh Edition, Joanne Hendrick.

*Refer to the **Self-Check Questions for Review.***

Chapter 13, p. 342.

focus for learning

Read this section before viewing the video program.

It is important to realize that it will be necessary for you to adjust to the variations in the cultural and ethnic backgrounds of the children you teach. Try to reflect on what you can do to honor ethnic differences and educate yourself on minority points of view.

Attempt to model nonsexist attitudes by taking the time to become aware of the way such attitudes permeate our lives. One excellent way to "raise your consciousness" about this is to do the **Observational Assignment** in this guide.

The video program, *Respecting Diversity,* can be a valuable tool in promoting thought and stimulating ideas for role-playing and practical experience. Use the following section of **Video-Related Questions** to help you begin to think about some of the important issues that the video program will address. That way, when similar questions are posed in the video, you can begin to think about what your responses might be. Being an active viewer of the video program will help you to respond to the following **Video-Related Questions for Reflection and Role Play** in a more meaningful way.

video-related questions for reflection and role play

Read these questions before viewing the video program. After viewing the program, respond to all these questions by interacting with another person, aloud to yourself or in your journal. Try to find opportunities to role play or practice the approaches illustrated.

1. In the video program, Dr. Hendrick says that children note differences between people's skin color and gender at a very early age. What can infant and toddler caregivers do to help very young children feel comfortable with people from different cultural or ethnic groups?

2. What are your ideas for comparative cultural activities that show the ways people from different cultures eat and sleep, as well as showing traditional housing, clothes and music? Try to develop activities that all children in a classroom can participate in and experience in order to share their traditions and learn about the traditions of others.

3. Try to find opportunities to role play interactions between children and teachers when children are asking about racial or ethnic differences and teachers are honestly and directly responding to their questions. Be sure that the "teacher" is using these exchanges as opportunities to provide positive information and possibly clear up any misconceptions the "children" may have.

4. How would you react to children teasing and making negative or even cruel comments about another's disability, skin color, sex or cultural heritage? Reflect on what your response might be in such a situation. Set up role playing interactions that would give you the opportunity to try out possible responses. It's important for the "teacher" to go beyond the negative comment and try to help the "attacker" discover the reason for his anger and make sure the "victim" in the situation gets the chance to respond.

5. What are some other similarities between children that teachers can emphasize in an effort to show how people are alike in fundamental ways, regardless of culture, disability or gender? Think of examples of biological and emotional needs that all people have in common, other than those mentioned in the video program.

6. What ideas do you have for non-traditional play activities for boys and girls, e.g., girls being physically active or boys working on fine-motor skills?

7. What experiences have you had with families sharing their cultural heritage with teachers and children in school? What ideas do you have for ways that families can help teachers and children learn about the clothes, food, music and stories that are part of their traditions?

8. Try to reflect on your own thoughts about racism and sexism. What attitudes have you encountered in other people or struggled with yourself in terms of racial or gender prejudice and stereotypes?

predicaments for your consideration

Respond to these predicaments with another person, aloud to yourself or in your journal.

1. You are a middle-class, white, well-meaning teacher, and you have just gotten a job working with a Head Start group in which the children are predominantly first-generation, in the U.S., Puerto Ricans. What will you do to make these children feel truly welcome? How can you utilize the rich cultural traditions of this minority group in your classroom?

   Now suppose that you could not serve Puerto Rican food, use their native dances or read books to the children about Puerto Rican children. What

uniqueness of these youngsters? Are there ways you might change to match the group you are serving more closely? Would changing yourself mean that you are losing your own cultural heritage?

2. A delegation of parents calls on you, the director, and says they want to discuss the racist policies of your school. In particular, they question the fact that all the teachers are white, and that all the aides are from minority groups. They have called a meeting for this evening and ask you to attend.

   What would be a desirable way to deal with this situation? Be sure to consider short- and long-term possibilities.

assignment for students working or volunteering with children

Complete this assignment and submit the written response to your instructor.

The purpose of this assignment is to prevent the development of prejudice against people from other cultures and races. It is most appropriate to do with 4- and 5-year-olds. This is accomplished by presenting something the child already knows about his own cultural background and linking that to something new from someone else's culture. *It is very important to make certain the children realize that doing something differently is not simply peculiar or strange.* Above all, try to avoid the nose wrinkling reaction, "Ugh! Imagine eating snails!" Instead, instill in them that "different" is interesting and valuable rather than to be disdained in a superior way. Cultivating this attitude also cultivates a wider one of general openness and willingness to venture, values we surely want to encourage in our children. In addition to appreciating different ways of meeting similar needs, we also want the children to see, over and over again, that all people have a great deal in common.

DEVELOP THE MULTICULTURAL ACTIVITY AREA

Create an activity area which involves a comparison between Anglo and some other culture. It might be between kinds of clothing, or beds used by Japanese and Western children, or different ways people bathe, or holidays that are similar or... ? Don't feel you should limit yourself to children abroad. It would be excellent to introduce a comparison with something from a specific Indian tribe (not a hodgepodge of "Indians") or from the Mexican American culture or from the culture of the African American people. Be accurate. You'll possibly have to do some reading on the subject, or ask advice from someone of the culture you are investigating.

(not a hodgepodge of "Indians") or from the Mexican American culture or from the culture of the African American people. Be accurate. You'll possibly have to do some reading on the subject, or ask advice from someone of the culture you are investigating.

On a nearby bulletin board, be sure you post an easy-to-read list of interesting facts the teachers using the activity area can share with the children about the activity. Avoid working too hard on elaborate bulletin boards. Also, be sure you list suggestions on how to use what is provided with the children so that they will have an enjoyable time there. This is the way positive emotions can be attached to their factual knowledge, and it is this positive feeling we are seeking to foster.

Remember, above all else, it must NOT be a museum presentation. It must be something the children can participate in and actually experience. You will probably want to add something to it during the week to keep the children from being bored with the same old thing by Friday.

WRITTEN ASSIGNMENT

1. Describe the activity area in some adequate way. Pictures, diagrams and written descriptions are all fine. Just make sure someone who has not seen it could understand what you did.

2. Include the lists of facts and suggestions you had posted in the activity area.

3. Describe how the children responded to the materials.

4. What evidence did you detect that they felt positively toward the culture as a result of your teaching activity?

5. When you do this in another classroom, what would you alter? What were the primary successes of the way you developed the activity?

6. If you were going to extend the experience, what would you do next?

observational assignment

Complete this assignment and submit the written response to your instructor.

The purpose of this assignment is to help you become more aware of television advertising and the "unnoticed" things it teaches that perpetuate sexist and racist attitudes.

Also, take careful note of whether any people from any other ethnic group than white appear, when they appear, that is, at what point in the commercial, and what they are doing.

Make a chart first and then check things off as they occur, with notes written at a place on the side. This avoids having to do a lot of rewriting and makes it possible to record data in an orderly way.

Take a look at the data when it has been completed and analyze it. On the basis of that data, what are commercials teaching children about who is important and what are appropriate roles for different ethnic groups and men and women to assume?

references for further reading

Beaty, J.J. (1997). *Building Bridges With Multicultural Picture Books for Children 3 to 5.* Upper Saddle River, NJ: Merrill/Prentice Hall.

Crawford, S. H. (1996). *Beyond Dolls and Guns: 101 Ways to Help Children Avoid Gender Bias.* Portsmouth, NH: Heinemann.

Derman-Sparks, L., & the ABC Task Force. (1989). *Anti-Bias Curriculum: Tools for Empowering Young Children.* Washington, DC: National Association for the Education of Young Children.

Ford, C.W. (1994). *We Can All Get Along: 50 Steps You Can Take to Help End Racism.* New York: Dell.

Lively, V., & Lively, E. (1991). *Sexual Development of Young Children.* Albany, NY: Delmar.

Schlank, C.H., & Metzger, B. (1997). *Together and Equal: Fostering Cooperative Play and Promoting Gender Equity in Early Childhood Programs.* Boston: Allyn & Bacon.

Shade, B.J., Kelly, C., & Oberg, M. (1997). *Creating Culturally Responsive Classrooms.* Washington, DC: American Psychological Association.

York, S. (1992). *Roots and Wings: Affirming Culture in Early Childhood Programs.* St. Paul, MN: Redleaf.

notes

unit 11
fostering creativity

video program: *creativity and play*

fostering creativity

unit overview

Read this section before reading the text assignment.

This unit on creativity is intended to widen your horizons so you see that creativity can be expressed in many modes and should be nourished accordingly. The basic principles of creativity are explored and the use of self-expressive materials are discussed in considerable detail. The importance of play in fostering creativity is emphasized in order to deepen your appreciation of the significance of this activity and to equip you with information so you will be able to defend the value of play to others when challenged. Since creativity is such an important aspect of play, this unit focuses on ways to foster freedom, imagination and spontaneity in play activity.

unit objectives

Read these objectives before reading the text assignment.

THIS UNIT:

1. Explains why creativity is so valuable in the life of children and why it is so important to nurture it.

2. Provides general recommendations about how to enhance creativity and specific recommendations for presenting various self-expressive creative activities.

3. Provides a wealth of reasons why play is essential in fostering the development of all selves of the child.

4. Recommends general ways teachers can support and extend creative play.

5. Provides practical suggestions for the development of play in specific circumstances.

text assignment

Read this assignment.

Chapter 14, "Fostering Creativity By Means Of Self-Expressive Materials" and Chapter 15, "Fostering Creativity In Play," *The Whole Child*, Seventh Edition, Joanne Hendrick.

Refer to the Self-Check Questions for Review.

Chapter 15, pp. 400-401.
Chapter 16, pp. 436-437.

focus for learning

Read this section before viewing the video program.

Actual experimentation with various creative materials will help you to become more comfortable working with these materials with young children. A dance demonstration that includes active participation will encourage you to include this kind of creative activity when working with preschool children.

Brief written observations of play activity can be used to identify the different functions play serves. Videotaped records of you working with children to facilitate play will also help you identify where you have been successful and where you may have dominated the activity or failed to step in at a moment when it might have been desirable to do so.

The video program, *Creativity and Play,* can be a valuable tool in promoting thought and stimulating ideas for role playing and practical experience. Use the following section of **Video-Related Questions** to help you begin to think about some of the important issues that the video program will address. That way, when similar questions are posed in the video program, you can begin to think about what your responses might be. Being an active viewer of the video program will help you to respond to the following **Video-Related Questions for Reflection and Role Play** in a more thoughtful way.

video-related questions for reflection and role play

Read these questions before viewing the video program. After viewing the program, respond to the questions assigned by your instructor by interacting with another person, aloud to yourself or in your journal. Try to find opportunities to role play or practice the approaches illustrated.

1. What ideas do students have for providing experiences that are based on the children's interests and ideas? What are the students' ideas for ways to understand the children's interests?

2. What difficulties and challenges have you experienced or can you envision in incorporating creative expression into early childhood programs? Reflect on possible scenarios you might find to be intimidating, e.g., how to respond to

a child's creative expression or a child's particularly challenging creative personality, the chaotic and often messy nature of creative activities or dealing with parental expectations of a "take-home product."

3. Try to brainstorm comments that would enhance children's creativity. Learn to ask thought-provoking questions that encourage children to continue to explore and involve themselves more deeply in their activities. Try to make comments about the pleasure the child is feeling as she works.

4. What factors would be important for teachers to consider when making creative activities available to children with disabilities? How can teachers give children with special needs the opportunity to take control and make independent choices about what they are doing?

5. Find opportunities to reflect on and discuss why you feel that play is such a worthwhile activity for young children. How can teachers resist the impulse to manipulate play experiences so the children "can really learn something" and allow children the freedom to develop their play in their own direction and at their own pace?

6. How can imaginative play foster intellectual development in young children? How can opportunities to experience and express their own interests and prior knowledge of the world help children to experiment, attempt and try out possibilities beyond their usual level of abilities? What would you say to a parent whose cultural heritage stresses high academic achievement from an early age and doesn't believe that play is at all related to intellectual development?

7. How can infant caregivers enhance social development through play with infants? How can preschool teachers encourage the development of social skills through dramatic play?

8. Find opportunities to role play ways to encourage creative play. Try to wait until the "children" express an interest, then ask how the "teacher" can help and what the "children" need. Attempt to extend the "children's" play by asking what will happen next, suggesting additional roles for bystanders and putting what the "children" are doing into words.

9. What ideas do you have for creative and unusual uses for standard equipment in child care centers?

predicaments for your consideration

Respond to the predicaments assigned by your instructor with another person, aloud to yourself or in your journal.

1. Chester, who is 3 years old, is new at school and has been watching the finger painting with considerable interest. At last he engages himself in this activity, only to discover to his horror that the purple paint has soaked right through his cotton smock onto his tee shirt. He is very concerned about this, particularly when the teacher is unable to wash all the paint out of the shirt, and his mother is genuinely angry when she picks him up that afternoon. How would you cope with this situation?

2. It is now February in your school, and the children seem to be doing an unusual amount of running about and getting into trouble. Pick two areas of your center, and explain how you would modify them to add interest and attract different children by changing the materials and equipment in some manner.

assignments for students working or volunteering with children

Complete the assignment(s) required by your instructor and submit the written response to him/her.

1. <u>A dance and movement assignment</u>

Select music and create an activity which helps children experience the pleasures of moving to music of all kinds and also to give them practice in relaxation, "letting their bodies go," during some portion of the activity. Be sure to use the children's ideas and spontaneous responses to the music. Use of accessories, such as scarves or streamers, helps children feel less self-conscious.

SUGGESTIONS

1. Try to do this activity at least once before you do it to write up. It will increase your chances of success and your confidence.

2. Be prepared to dance with the children.

3. Familiarize yourself with the music in advance. Select a range of mood and tempo so the children can be encouraged to move and do what the music suggests to them. Include folk music from the various cultures of the children.

4. Avoid the use of instruments with this experience. This is not meant to be a rhythm band experience.

WRITTEN ASSIGNMENT

1. Give an overall description of how the activity went and your evaluation of its success. Be sure to include reasons why you judged it as being successful or needing to improve.

2. Tell how you gathered the children in and how you began the activity.

3. Explain which of your own ideas you used and which ideas the children contributed.

4. Describe the relaxation experience you offered and whether it was effective.

2. <u>Assignment for enhancing creativity in play</u>

There are many ways of helping children have creative ideas as they play. The skill lies in providing equipment, suggesting possibilities and keeping your ears attentively open to the children's ideas so that you can be their supporter not their leader. It involves offering support and suggestions they are free to refuse and staying open to possibilities as the children develop them. Creativity in play is most frequently expressed through the unusual use of equipment and through dramatic pretend play. The basic point is that the children are using their minds to do some pretending and imagining excellent cognitive work as well as being excellent clarifiers of emotional problems and situations.

ASSIGNMENT WITH THE CHILDREN

Assemble something for the children to use that you feel will entice them into creative play and ask the children what they would like to do with it. Your creation might be related in some way to an interest the children are pursuing or it might involve combining equipment in a fresh way. The creative play idea for this assignment must come from the children.

Two year olds are going to need simplicity and more structure than the 3 and 4 year olds will need. Keep your eyes open and capitalize on the children's creative ideas. Work on how you can enhance any dramatic role playing that develops.

WRITTEN ASSIGNMENT

1. Describe what took place during the creative play activity. Be sure to include the names of those who participated, how the activity shifted and changed during the period and how equipment was added or changed during the play. Identify clearly the children's creative behavior and ideas.

2. Briefly explain why you anticipated that the things you provided would generate creative play among the children or by an individual child.

3. Describe something you did during play that promoted positive social interaction between the children.

4. If you were your head teacher, what suggestions would you give yourself about how to help the children be more creative next time you offer them this kind of opportunity?

observational assignments

Complete the assignment(s) chosen by your instructor and submit your written response to him/her.

1. Make arrangements to observe children in a preschool classroom working on a project using creative materials, such as paint, dough or collage. The intention of this assignment is to help you think about ways to foster creative self-expression in children. Look for use of free-form materials or variations on classic materials.

WRITTEN ASSIGNMENT

1. Describe what the project was and how children responded to it.

2. How well did the activity encourage creative self-expression among the children?

3. What, if anything, did the teacher do to intentionally make this a creative experience for the children?

4. Did anything happen that may have deadened the self-expressiveness of the children? If so, please discuss.

5. What would you do to improve the presentation of this type of material?

2. Make arrangements to observe children in the block area of a preschool classroom. The intention of this assignment is to help you think of ways to generate creative block play on a long-term basis (more than one day) by adding accessories or combining materials in an unusual way.

WRITTEN ASSIGNMENT

1. What, if any, accessories were used in the block area that you observed? How did they encourage creative play? Were any accessories added as a result of the way that the play developed?

2. Did the teacher do anything else to encourage block play besides setting out interesting materials?

3. How were the children drawn into the play?

4. How was clean-up handled by the teacher? Did the children cooperate in putting the blocks away?

5. Given the same situation, what would you do to encourage creative block play with these children? What different materials would you add or combine? What comments would you make in response to the direction of their play? How would you draw interested children into the play?

references for further reading

Chenfeld, M. B. (1995). *Creative Activities for Young Children* (2nd ed.). Orlando, FL: Harcourt Brace.

Greenman, J. (1998). *Places for Childhoods: Making Quality Happen in the Real World.* Redmond, WA: Exchange Press.

Hendrick, J.B. (Ed.). (1997). *First Steps Toward Teaching the Reggio Way.* Upper Saddle River, NJ: Merrill/Prentice Hall.

Hirsch, E.S. (Ed.). (1996). *The Block Book* (3rd ed.). Washington, DC: National Association for the Education of Young Children.

Isenberg, J.P. & Jalongo, M.R. (1997). *Creative Expression and Play in the Early Childhood Curriculum* (2nd ed.). Upper Saddle River, NJ: Merrill/Prentice Hall.

MacDonald, S. (1996). *Squish, Sort, Paint & Build: Over 200 Easy Learning Center Activities.* Beltsville, MD: Gryphon House.

Schirrmacher, R. (1998). *Art and Creative Development for Young Children* (3rd ed.). Albany, NY: Delmar.

unit 12
fostering the development
of language skills and
emergent literacy

video program: *let's talk about it*

fostering the development of language skills and emergent literacy

unit overview

Read this section before reading the text assignment.

This unit explains how language is acquired and then sets forth some basic principles of language instruction in the preschool that will increase the children's competence in this vital area. It also discusses the question of bilingualism and language disabilities that commonly occur among preschool children. The unit then considers the pressures preschool teachers are likely to feel from administrators and parents to present highly structured reading programs and suggests ways to cope with those pressures. Emergent literacy is defined as it relates to reading, writing and mathematics, and ways to foster its growth are explored. The unit concludes with advice about how to present successful group times that foster the growth of literacy.

unit objectives

Read these objectives before reading the text assignment.

This unit:

1. Discusses various theories of language acquisition and outlines the stages of language development for young children.

2. Provides you with six basic ways to foster language development.

3. Informs you about the significance and value of language and dialectical differences.

4. Recommends methods of working with children who have specific language disorders.

5. Discusses ways to cope with pressures to present highly structured reading programs to preschool children.

6. Defines emergent literacy and provides practical ways to incorporate developmentally appropriate literacy-based materials in the preschool curriculum.

7. Discusses methods of conducting group times that foster both language development and group harmony.

text assignment

Read this assignment.

Chapter 16, "Fostering the Development of Language Skills" and Chapter 17, "Fostering the Emergence of Literacy," *The Whole Child*, Seventh Edition, Joanne Hendrick.

Refer to the Self-Check Questions for Review.

Chapter 16, pp. 435-436.
Chapter 17, p. 460.

focus for learning

Read this section before viewing the video program.

It is important for you to develop the ability to differentiate between children who have serious developmental problems in language ability and more typical children. Therefore, it will help you to learn the developmental stages associated with the growth of language and to identify symptoms that signal the child needs special help.

An additional way to heighten your power of perception is to formulate your own checklist for language development and use this with several children to estimate the children's level of development.

Be prepared to face pressures to use developmentally inappropriate materials when working in the language/cognitive area of development. Actual practice in answering such suggestions is the most effective way of doing this. Reflecting on the pros and cons of early reading will also help you do what's best for the children.

The video program, *Let's Talk About It*, can be a valuable tool in promoting thought and stimulating ideas for role-playing and practical experience. Use the following section of **Video-Related Questions** to help you begin to think about some of the important issues that the video program will address. That way, when similar questions are posed in the video, you can begin to think about what your responses might be. Being an active viewer of the video program will help you to respond to the following **Video-Related Questions for Reflection and Role Play** in a more meaningful way.

video-related questions for reflection and role play

Read these questions before viewing the video program. After viewing the program, respond to all these questions by interacting with another person, aloud to yourself or in your journal. Try to find opportunities to role play or practice the approaches illustrated.

1. What ideas do you have for communicating with infants? When and how would you talk to an infant in your care? How would you show you are listening and how would you get the baby to respond?

2. Try to find opportunities to role play conducting a true conversation with a child. Be sure that the "teacher" is listening with sincere interest, responding in a way that will continue the conversation and waiting for the "child" to answer. What are some examples of real and relevant subjects that children in a child care environment can talk about? What kind of problem-solving situations could be a part of conversations between children?

3. Brainstorm examples of open-ended questions that teachers could ask children in a preschool setting. Be sure these questions are designed to engage the children in dialogue and sharing ideas.

4. What experience have you had with bilingual children? What ideas do you have for helping a bilingual child and her family to feel comfortable at school?

5. Find opportunities to think about or discuss the concept of "emergent literacy." Be sure you thoroughly understand the interactive and participatory nature of this way of learning.

6. What are possible causes of language delay in a young child? Be sure you understand the range of reasons that a child may be slow to talk. Where in your community could such a child be referred, depending on the cause of the language disorder?

predicaments for your consideration

Respond to these predicaments with another person, aloud to yourself or in your journal.

1. You are teaching a class of 4 year olds and a new little girl named Rosa joined the group last month. She speaks only Spanish as does her mother and, as far as you know, her father. You speak only English as does your assistant teacher. Six weeks after enrolling she is still crying miserably every time her mother departs and she spends the rest of the morning sitting in the book corner as far away from the other children and you as she can get. She just

sits there, looking down at her hands until her mother returns. She shakes her head when invited to snack and also refuses to go outside with the other children.

What could you do to help Rosa feel more comfortable in the classroom? What ideas do you have for communicating with Rosa and her mother?

2. The mother of a child in your group glows as she tells you her 3 year old is so smart, he knows all his ABCs and his father is drilling him every night with flash cards to help him learn to read. What, if anything, do you think you should do about this?

3. A house close to your children's center recently burned down, and the children are both interested and concerned about what happened. For this reason, you have decided it would be useful to provide some firefighter props to help them clarify their understanding about what happened. You would like to include a number of literacy-type materials along with the other equipment. Suggest several items that could be included that might encourage children to engage in emergent literacy-related play.

assignments for students working or volunteering with children

Complete these assignments and submit the written response to your instructor.

1. <u>Plan and run a set of group time activities with children.</u>

Overall goals of this assignment are to help you:

1. suit group time to the interests, attention span and developmental level of the particular children in that particular group,

2. integrate the group time experience with whatever interest is currently being pursued by the children, and

3. realize that a good group time has variety, although no one group is likely to cover all the following seven areas. For the purposes of this assignment, all seven should be included in the plan (stories, poetry and finger plays, auditory training, songs, discussion and a cognitive game, and a multiethnic and a nonsexist component). Include all these in the plan, but resign yourself to using some of them during this group time and the rest another time.

WRITTEN ASSIGNMENT

1. List the names and ages of the children in the group and how long the group time lasted.

2. Devise a simple, four-column chart that lists the materials you planned to use that fulfill each of the seven areas. List and identify the area and specific activity in the first column. In the second column, give the reason for including that item. Next, tell whether you used it and finally, in the fourth column, evaluate the item used.

2. <u>Plan and run a set of book and music activities with children.</u>

The purpose of this assignment is to encourage you to provide an integrated story and singing time. Since you've read many stories to the children already, you will be building on existing skills and increasing your abilities in this area. Repeat the activities on a second day. Try to weave the stories and songs together. Use the same two songs both days, but vary the books.

BOOK ASSIGNMENT

Acquire three good, age-appropriate children's books from the library or bookmobile. Get them from the library rather than using books available at school so that you have a fresh source to choose from. This will cause you to exercise more careful judgment and provide variety for the children as well. Before picking out the books, decide what age you will be reading to. Think of particular children who will be in the group and check with the master teacher about special areas the group will be working on at this time, such as "boats," "worms" or possibly some kind of field trip or theme. Try to suit your selections to these three criteria (age, special needs of individual children and interest). At least one of the books must be about children from another culture. Using the standards in Appendix C in the text, eliminate any books that have racist or sexist overtones.

For each book, turn in an analysis that includes the following points:

1. Bibliographical reference (title, author, date and place of publication and publisher).

2. Brief summary of story (two or three sentences).

3. An evaluation of the quality of the book:
   a. literary quality (classic? well written? hard to understand? award winner?).
   b. pictorial quality (beautiful? dull?)

4. The age level it fit.

5. Whether it was at the right age and interest level for the children in your group.

6. Whether the children liked it. (Ask them.)

7. Whether it promoted discussion between you and the children.

   a. Were there opportunities for the children to talk about the story and pictures?

   b. How did you get the children to participate rather than just sitting quietly and listening?

8. Would you use the book again? Why or why not?

9. Identify any book you discarded as being racist or sexist and explain, using specific examples, why you felt this to be true.

MUSIC ASSIGNMENT

1. List two songs you taught the children during the book-music assignment.

2. List any weak points about the song or your presentation and what you would do to improve this next time.

3. List the strengths of each song. Please be more sophisticated than simply asserting that the children just loved it.

4. Do you think each song would be worth using again? Explain why or why not.

observational assignment

Complete this assignment and submit the written response to your instructor.

Make arrangements to observe in a preschool classroom for at least half a day. Observe the children during free play and try to determine what their current interests are. Listen to their conversations and pay attention to their play. Take notes on your observations.

Plan a group time for this class, taking into consideration what you heard and observed. Integrate this experience with whatever interests are currently being pursued by the children by planning activities that further explore these interests. Be sure to suit the group time to the developmental level of the children in that classroom. Include the following seven areas in your plan: stories, poetry and finger plays, auditory training, songs, discussion and a cognitive game, and a multiethnic and a nonsexist component.

WRITTEN ASSIGNMENT

1. Write a summary of your observations in the classroom including the age group observed, what you perceived their interests to be and why.

2. For each of the seven areas, list the materials you would use and your reason for using them. How would each activity contribute to further exploration of the subject areas that interest these children?

references for further reading

Arbuthnot, M.H., & Root, S.L. (1968). *Time for Poetry* (3rd ed.). Glenview, IL: Scott, Foresman.

Bos, B. (1983). *Before the Basics: Creating Conversations With Children.* Roseville, CA: Turn the Page Press.

Carroll, D.W. (1999). *Psychology of Language* (3rd ed.). Pacific Grove, CA: Brooks/Cole.

Moomaw, S. (1997). *More Than Singing: Discovering Music in Preschool and Kindergarten.* St. Paul, MN: Redleaf.

Oyer, H.J., & Hall, B.J. (1994). *Speech, Language, and Hearing Disorders: A Guide for Teachers.* Boston: College Hill.

Redleaf, R. (1993). *Busy Fingers, Growing Minds: Fingerplays, Verses, and Activities for Whole Language Learning.* St Paul, MN: Readleaf.

Shade, D.D., & Davis, B.S. (1997). The Role of Computer Technology in Early Childhood Education. In J.P. Isenberg & M.R. Jalongo (Eds.), *Major Trends and Issues in Early Childhood Education: Challenges, Controversies, and Insights.* New York: Teachers College Press.

unit 13
developing thinking and
reasoning skills

video program: *growing minds*

developing thinking and reasoning skills

unit overview

Read this section before reading the text assignment.

This unit stresses basic, humanistic learning priorities in order to help you to understand the importance of developing children's cognitive selves at an appropriate level and through suitable methods. These priorities include maintaining the child's sense of wonder and curiosity, keeping cognitive learning a source of genuine pleasure, binding it to affective experience whenever possible and accompanying it with language.

Piaget's basic concepts are described and their relevance to children's learning is explained. A practical description of various mental abilities is provided. These include the ability to match identical items, group items according to their common properties, arrange items in logical order, perceive common relationships between items, begin to grasp the principle of conservation and think about simple cause-and-effect relationships.

Some basic ways teachers can encourage young children to think creatively and produce original ideas are presented. Emphasis is on understanding the concept of convergent/divergent thinking and upon using the inquiry method as a means of stimulating thought. The most relevant concepts of Vygotsky are introduced and the virtues of emergent curriculum as exemplified by the preschools of Reggio Emilia, Italy, are explored. Clear distinctions are made between using fact, figuring-out and creative questions, and suggestions are made for how to use creative questions most effectively. Basic principles to employ when using the emergent approach are discussed, stressing the value of language, being sensitive to the children's genuine interests and keeping these explorations focused.

unit objectives

Read these objectives before reading the text assignment.

THIS UNIT:

1. Identifies and describes the most important underlying priorities when planning learning activities for the cognitive self.

2. Discusses contributions of the cognitive theorist, Piaget.

3. Explains the value of developing specific mental abilities when teaching young children and recommends appropriate activities.

4. Provides you with techniques that make it easier to use thought-provoking questions.

5. Clarifies how the emergent approach differs from and enhances the conventional approach to cognitive curriculum.

6. Describes the elements of the emergent approach and explains how to put it into practice.

text assignment

Read this assignment.

Chapter 18, "Developing Thinking and Reasoning Skills: Using the Emergent Approach To Foster Creativity in Thought," and Chapter 19, "Developing Thinking and Reasoning Skills: Using the Conventional Approach To Build Midlevel Mental Abilities," *The Whole Child*, Seventh Edition, Joanne Hendrick.

*Refer to the **Self-Check Questions for Review**.*

Chapter 18, pp. 489-490.
Chapter 19, p. 520.

focus for learning

Read this section before viewing the video program.

If you are currently working with children, it will be beneficial to list topics of interest that arose spontaneously from the children's concerns and then reflect or discuss possibilities for development. It's important to understand the difference between the conventional approach which focuses on midlevel mental ability skills and the emergent approach.

Find opportunities to practice developing activities that foster the growth of specific mental abilities by trying out these activities with children. Making a schedule that integrates midlevel thinking and reasoning experiences into the daily life of the school in a practical way will also contribute to your

schedule that integrates midlevel thinking and reasoning experiences into the daily life of the school in a practical way will also contribute to your understanding of the use of the conventional approach to cognitive development.

Comparing divergent and convergent teaching techniques by acting them out will help you clarify these concepts in your own mind. Focus on the idea of allowing cognitive curriculum to emerge gradually as the children's interests develop while keeping the direction of it focused.

The video program, *Growing Minds,* can be a valuable tool in promoting thought and stimulating ideas for role-playing and practical experience. Use the following section of **Video-Related Questions** to help you begin to think about some of the important issues that the video program will address. That way, when similar questions are posed in the video, you can begin to think about what your responses might be. Being an active viewer of the video program will help you to respond to the following **Video-Related Questions for Reflection and Role Play** in a more meaningful way.

video-related questions for reflection and role play

Read these questions before viewing the video program. After viewing the program, respond to all these questions by interacting with another person, aloud to yourself or in your journal. Try to find opportunities to role play or practice the approaches illustrated.

1. How can you, as an infant caregiver, help the children in your care to feel valued? How can you show parents how to express to their infants that they value them?

2. What experiences have you had with the "emergent" approach to teaching and learning? Have you experienced classrooms where the children's interests were considered when planning activities? Have you experienced teachers and children solving problems and coming up with solutions together? Reflect on your experiences and your feelings about them.

3. Find an opportunity to role play an interaction with a parent when the teacher is being asked what the children are learning during a particular activity. You can use activities from your experiences in preschool classrooms as examples or activities that you have seen in the video program. Be sure the "teacher" is explaining what thinking skills the children are using, encouraging the "parent" to visit the classroom and contribute his suggestions as well.

4. What do you think the connection is between being successful at learning and feeling good about one's self?

5. Find an opportunity to role play ways to respond to children who ask questions in order to help them to figure out their own answers. What are the best ways to respond that will help the children move from one thought to another and solve their own problems or challenges?

6. Why do you think that field trips and other hands-on experiences are excellent opportunities to learn for children? What experiences have you had with field trips and ways that children and teachers continued exploring topics back in the classroom?

7. Find the opportunity to practice asking "open-ended questions" that would provoke children into thinking for themselves and encourage them to think of original ideas. You can use scenes from the video program or your own experiences and brainstorm thought-provoking questions to ask about these activities.

predicaments for your consideration

Respond to these predicaments with another person, aloud to yourself or in your journal.

1. One of the 3 year olds in your room notices some bird tracks in the snow when the children go out to play. Suggest some spontaneous activities you could do with her that would encourage her to interact with the snow and to investigate further how the bird tracks were made. Now demonstrate that you understand the difference DeVries and Kohlberg draw between active involvement and more passive interest by suggesting a couple of things you could do that would cause the child to not take action herself.

   On that same snowy day, the children are fascinated with the snow itself because it's the first snow of winter. What are some activities you could do with them that would provide some learning while remaining real fun for the children? Be sure to identify what the children would be learning and why you think they will enjoy the experiences.

2. The children are very excited when they arrive at school because the previous night their town has been shaken by a moderate earthquake. Although it did not appear to do any permanent damage, it recalls to mind the prior experience of the much more severe earthquake the children underwent about this time last year.

It is obvious the topic has great relevancy to their lives so you decide to follow the children's interests and encourage curriculum to emerge around this subject. Suggest some possible directions the pathway might follow as the subject develops. What problems can you think up concerning earthquakes that could provoke the children into explanations and solutions. Be sure to include some examples of ways you could bind the affective (feelings) part of the curriculum to this cognitive learning.

3. You have in your room a little girl about 3 years old who asks a lot of questions. For example, she might ask, "Why are we going in now?" When provided with the reasons, she then asks, "But why?" If you were her teacher, would you think this type of inquiry should be encouraged? How would you handle it?

assignments for students working or volunteering with children

Complete these assignments and submit the written response to your instructor.

1. This assignment is designed to help you learn to develop a topic based on the children's interests. Be alert to what interests the children or a particular child during the coming week and build the following assignment around that interest.

WRITTEN ASSIGNMENT

1. Describe the interest you identified and explain how it arose from the children.

2. Then imagine you were actually thinking of using that interest as a topic for developing cognitive curriculum. Provide at least one practical thing you would do to:

a. Continue the children's curiosity about the subject.

b. Make investigation of the subject pleasureable for you and the children.

c. Include feelings as part of the learning experience.

d. Include ways the children can show what they have learned by using language in some form and using some other form of graphic expression as well.

2. The purpose of this assignment is to sensitize you to the innumerable possibilities for creative thinking and problem solving that come up every day in preschool once you are alert to them.

    Devise a number of provocations (problems) for the children to think about and ask them how they would solve them. Examples of provocations range from "Where could we put the fish while we clean the aquarium?" to "What shall we do? There are only three crackers left and five of us want them?"

    It will be helpful to write questions and answers down as they occur during the day in order not to forget them, or use a tape recorder. Do your best to take advantage of spontaneous provocations as well as the more contrived questions you thought up in advance.

    WRITTEN ASSIGNMENT

    Write up two examples describing the situation and the provocation and answer the following questions for each.

    1. Was it a spontaneous or pre-thought-out provocation?
    2. What question(s) did you ask?
    3. Did you provide "wait time" after asking the question(s)?
    4. What were the replies? Was there more than one answer?
    5. Were you able to put the solutions into use?

observational assignment

Complete this assignment and submit the written response to your instructor.

The purpose of this assignment is to help you clarify your understanding of the various mental abilities discussed in the text. It also will provide you with a nice supply of learning materials to use with the children.

FINISHED ASSIGNMENT

1. Create a set of activities for children which encourage each of the following mental abilities: grouping, matching, common relations, temporal ordering, seriation and cause and effect.

2. Each activity must have enough material for six children to participate. That is, if you were making a lotto game you would need to make six lotto boards.

3. Make a storage box for each activity. Make these boxes neat looking because they will be sitting out on a shelf.

4. Make a description card to go with each activity which includes:

   a. The name of the activity, which mental ability it is intended for and a definition of the ability.

   b. A description of how you would present it to make it fun for the children to use. It is very important to present these materials in an appealing way.

   c. A description of how you would present it to 2 year olds and how you would present it to 4 year olds. That is, the description card should explain how to make the activity simple and easy and how to make it more challenging.

   d. An explanation of why this mental ability is a useful "preacademic" skill for children to acquire.

5. Make at least two of the items three dimensional. Don't depend only on pictures and flannel boards. Children need things to handle, investigate and manipulate.

references for further reading

Baum, S.E., & Cray-Andrews, M. (1983). *Creativity 1, 2, 3*. New York: Trillium Press.

Cadwell, L.B. (1997). *Bringing Reggio Emilia Home: An Innovative Approach to Early Childhood Education*. New York: Teachers College Press.

Devries, R., & Zan, B. (1994). *Moral Children, Moral Classrooms: Creating a Constructivist Atmosphere in Early Education*. New York: Teachers College Press.

Graves, M. (1998). *Planning Around Children's Interests: The Teacher's Idea Book 2*. Ypsilanti, MI: High/Scope.

Hendrick, J.B. (Ed.). (1997). *First Steps Toward Teaching the Reggio Way*. Upper Saddle River, NJ: Merrill/Prentice Hall.

Moomaw, S., & Hieronymous, B. (1995). *More Than Counting: Whole Math Activities for Preschool and Kindergarten*. St. Paul, MN: Redleaf.

Shore, R. (1997). *Rethinking the Brain: New Insights Into Early Development*. New York: Families and Work Institute. Also available from National Association for the Education of Young Children.

Singer, D.G., & Revenson, T.A. (1997). *A Piaget Primer: How a Child Thinks* (Rev. ed.). Madison, CT: International Universities Press.

notes